FIRST, FIRST, . . . AND BRIEFEST

ELKANAH AND SARAH MACKEY: THE 1856 PRESBYTERIAN MISSION TO THE BLACKFOOT INDIANS

James Howard Trott

Oak and Yew Press
Philadelphia

FIRST, FIRST, . . . AND BRIEFEST

Elkanah and Sarah Mackey: The 1856 Presbyterian Mission To the Blackfoot Indians

An account of the first Protestant missionary
and his wife, the "first white woman"
to reach Fort Benton, Montana.

James Howard Trott

Elkanah Dare and Sarah Armstrong Mackey

CONTENTS

Introduction

In 1856, Elkanah and Sarah Mackey, the two young newlyweds from Pennsylvania, shown on the cover and frontispiece, left their familiar homes, families and communities, to travel into the Far West as Christian missionaries. This couple were bound for the northern plains and what is now Montana to tell Blackfoot Indians about Jesus. This mission, carried forward by the Presbyterian Church, was set in motion by a letter from another Pennsylvanian. Alexander Culbertson was a fur trader, and the head of the American Fur Company post at Fort Benton, deep in the remote wilderness, and was himself married to a Blackfoot woman.

What inspired Alexander Culbertson late in his frontier career to initiate his "call" to the Presbyterians for a Blackfoot Mission?

What kind of motives did the first Protestant missionaries have – she, the first "white woman" to arrive at that rough outpost of Fort Benton [1] -- in answering that call? Why would a young Princeton graduate and his brand-new bride set out for that incomplete adobe fort so remote on the "headwaters of the Missouri River," more than a thousand miles beyond any place then considered "civilized"?

A variety of motives seem to emerge as the story unfolds, but we would be remiss to neglect the ancient and powerful motive of most Christian missions for the last two thousand years.

---

[1] No steamboats had gone that far up in 1856. Yet within the next decades Fort Benton was to become "the head port of navigation" on the Missouri, with remarkably large boats making their way there from St. Louis – the farthest inland port for large boats in the entire world. The first steamboat arrived in Benton in 1859.

Whatever else they may say about them, most historians agree the American colonies began self-consciously as Christian settlements. These colonies had more than their share of mixed motives, insane wars and witch-hunts. No one who knows their history can deny the New England colonists exhibited zealous religious intolerance -- especially toward others claiming to worship the same Savior with different shades of doctrine. But at the very beginning, and over again frequently along the way, the colonists made formal statements to the effect that they believed themselves to have been given a special commission. That commission was to bring the Christian message to the natives of this continent.

Thus the *First Charter of Virginia* (Jamestown, April 10, 1606)

> We, greatly commending, and graciously accepting of, their Desires for the Furtherance of so noble a Work, which may, by the Providence of Almighty God, hereafter tend to the Glory of His Divine Majesty, in propagating of Christian Religion to such People, as yet live in Darkness and miserable Ignorance of the true Knowledge and Worship of God, and may in time bring the Infidels and Savages, living in those Parts, to human Civility, and to a settled and quiet Government.

Thus the *Mayflower Compact* (1620):

> . . . Having undertaken, for the glory of God, and advancement of the Christian faith, and honor of our King and Country, a voyage to plant the first colony in the northern parts of Virginia [Massachusetts], do by these presents solemnly and mutually, in the presence of God, and one of another, covenant and combine our selves together into a civil body politic, for our better ordering and preservation and furtherance of the ends aforesaid. . .

Thus the *New England Charter* (1620): ". . . to advance the enlargement of Christian religion, to the glory of God Almighty . . . ."

Thus the official seal of Massachusetts Bay Colony (1629), which depicted an Indian appealing, "Come over and help us".

Thus the life-long dedication of such monumental men as John Eliot "The Apostle to the Indians," and David Brainerd, son-in-law to the famous Jonathan Edwards. At least a minority continued to carry that fervor into the new-found and re-organized nation known as the United States.

European zeal for "foreign missions" continued to provide a motive for later immigrants. The Moravians and various German Anabaptist groups came with a sense of religious mission. At the frontiers, especially, there were always missionaries among the white settlers who were excited about reaching "the Indians".

George Whitefield, perhaps the greatest evangelist of American history, went back and forth from England to America, and up and down through all the American colonies from 1738 through 1770 (dying at last while struggling to preach) on four major evangelistic tours. Most historians recognize the cohesive power his preaching had among the colonists, and the tremendous increase of Christian zeal wherever he went.

Then early in the 1800's, a revival of interest in foreign missions flamed up at Williams College and Andover Newton Theological Seminary in Massachusetts. The original zeal to reach Native Americans resurged throughout the early nineteenth century. Various denominations sent missionaries to tribes and peoples thousands of miles from permanent settlements.

The American Board of Commissioners for Foreign Missions was founded in 1810, and by 1812 its first missionaries were going to the Indians. There was an amazing willingness to go the limit – to the point of death as in the case of the Whitmans and Spauldings. But there were other kinds of sacrifice willingly entered into, as in the cases of the several missionaries arrested and jailed by the State of Georgia in 1831, when they refused to abandon the Cherokees to facilitate Georgia's invasion of their lands.

Michael Simpson Culbertson,
China Missionary and Alexander's brother

Caught up in this zeal for "foreign missions" (for Chinese and Native Americans were both regarded as "foreign" insofar as missions efforts of the time) were two

Pennsylvania families, important to this story. Both families were Presbyterian. Both were to send sons (with their families) into the "darkest" and most distant parts of the world.

Michael Simpson Culbertson left his hometown of Chambersburg, PA, at the age of sixteen (1835) to go to West Point. He graduated in 1839, and after two years of service, resigned his commission to go to Princeton Seminary, from which he graduated in 1844. Thereupon, he and his new wife became early members of a stream of Christian men and women embarking as missionaries to China. There most of them (and many of their children) eventually became martyrs to the faith.

James Love Mackey, himself an educator from the age of fourteen, studied and taught at various academies in and near his home town of New London, in Chester County, PA. He, too, went on to graduate from Princeton Seminary and be ordained, in 1849. Along with his young wife, Elizabeth J. Blair and another couple named Simpson[2], he sailed to West Africa for the sake of the gospel.

These two, Michael Culbertson and James Mackey, each had a brother who was a principal character in the story of the 1856 Blackfoot Mission of the Presbyterian Board of Foreign Missions.

---

[2] Note Michael Culbertson's middle name – was his family related to these Simpsons? Michael was known as "Simpson" throughout much of his life as a missionary.

60 THE FOREIGN MISSIONARY

Miscellany.

INDIANS HUNTING BUFFALOES.

THOUSANDS of buffaloes are to be found in the western country—the country lying beyond the settlements of white people, and extending to the Rocky Mountains. They afford food to many of the savage Indians, and their skins are dressed by Indian traders, and sold in most of our towns and cities. The poor animals, indeed, are killed chiefly for their skins; and no doubt many of our young readers have often been kept warm in winter, while sleigh riding or travelling in other ways, by nice buffalo robes, which passed through the hands of Indians and Indian traders in the far west. This little picture shows how the Indians sometimes kill the buffalo. It is said that there is often great danger from the herds of buffaloes. When excited, they rush with headlong fury across the vast plains, and woe betide everything that comes in their way. The Indian, with characteristic cunning, approaches them in disguise, as they are quietly grazing, unsuspicious of danger; and shoots down with his arrows one after another, without alarming the vast herd.

The buffaloes are said to be diminishing in numbers. The advance of civilization contracts the range of their pasture. The demand for their robes consigns thousands of them every year to death. Soon this noble animal will have disappeared. Is he not a type of the poor Indian, his inveterate foe?

Yet there is a hope for the Indian. He possesses a soul, which is capable of the noblest culture, and of the highest happiness.

Preach the Gospel to the Indians. Teach the Gospel to their children. Foster the Indian Mission Schools. Then will the decay of this interesting people be arrested. Christianity first, and afterwards civilization, will multiply their numbers and adorn their dwellings. Hope and eternal life will take the place of discouragement and death. No longer will the Indian seek a precarious subsistence with his bow and arrows; but he will be a comfortable farmer, or a skilful mechanic, or a successful merchant, or an honored professional man—perhaps a Senator, or a Governor, or a President, and, especially, in many instances, a faithful minister of the Gospel. Such will be the fruits of Missions among the Indians!

Brief article in *The Foreign Missionary*
Presbyterian missions magazine, 1856

CHAPTER ONE - Preparing for Mission

Alexander Culbertson was born in 1809, ten years earlier than his half-brother[3] Michael, and showed little evidence of missionary zeal. He left Pennsylvania in 1826, going with an uncle who served as a military "sutler" to troops in Florida. Within a few years, Alexander wandered farther afield to St. Louis and the western wilderness. From there, beginning when he was only twenty years old, he began to travel far and wide as an employee, then foreman of western fur companies. He became a respected trader, then "factor" or "bourgeois", that is, head trader at Fort Benton, (in what is now Montana). He married a Blackfoot woman "Natawista" at Fort Union about 1840[4] and they made their permanent home in Illinois. From there they regularly returned to Fort Benton.

James Mackey's brother, on the other hand, attended Princeton College, then followed his brother

---

[3] Joseph Culbertson of Chambersburg, PA was their father, but Alexander was third son of his first wife, Mary Finley, while Michael was the first son of his second wife, Frances Stuart. The roots of all these families and their community were Scottish and Presbyterian.
[4] Jack Holterman, *King of the High Missouri,* Local tradition at Fort Benton has Father De Smet marrying these two at one of the fur posts - but according to Holterman's sources, they were married more or less according to Blackfoot traditions in 1840 or 41, and were not married by European rites until 9 Sep 1859, on which occasion Father Thomas Scanlon of St. Joseph officiated. Alexander indicated to his friends that he arranged this for the purpose of rendering his children's status legitimate under U.S. law and thus guaranteeing their legal rights.

James's path through Princeton Seminary. Elkanah Dare Mackey , son of William and Sarah (Martin) Mackey, was born in Pennsylvania, in Colerain township [5], Lancaster county, on September 16, 1826. This family like the Culbertsons, was of Scotch-Irish descent, and included his older brother, James Love, one younger brother, William Downey, and a sister Jane (later Jane M. Kelso) beside two more of whom we shall speak later.

Elkanah Dare Mackey was named for Elkanah Kelsey Dare [6] the first pastor of the Colerain Presbyterian Church. [7]

The Mackey's were firm Presbyterians. Many of their ancestors were persecuted as "Covenanters" in Scotland - Martins and Guthries as well as Mackeys. They had a history of standing on principle. During the period of our narrative, some of them had taken a stand on the issue of slavery:

> In 1845 the General Assembly of the Presbyterian Church of the United States made a deliverance on the subject of slavery. Fifteen ministers of the churches located in Western Pennsylvania and Ohio seceded from the church because of the pro-slavery sentiments of the Assembly's utterance. Certain members of the Presbyterian Churches of Union, Oxford, Fagg's Manor, and Octorara sympathized with these ministers and erected a church building, and effected an organization called the Free Presbyterian Church of Colerain. This

---

[5] Coleraine like nearby Rapho was named for the place in Ireland its early settlers came from. *A Brief History of Lancaster County,*. by Israel Smith Clare. Edited By Anna Lyle, Millersville State Normal School. Lancaster, PA:, Argus Pub. Co.,1892., p 125.

[6] Apparently Elkanah Dare was friends with both Alexander Hamilton and Benjamin Franklin. Phone conversation with Marty Greenleaf, 15 June 2016, in which he referred to a published Union Church history.

[7] This congregation is now Union Presbyterian Church of Kirkwood, PA.

building is located in Colerain township, near Andrew's Bridge. It is still standing , and is used as a public hall. This church was dissolved at the request of its members April 14, 1874 by the Presbytery of Westminster and the members transferred to Union Church. [8]

Sarah Martin Mackey, Elkanah's mother

[8] *History of Lancaster County : with Biographical sketches. . .*by Franklin Ellis and Samuel Evans Phila, 1883, p. 733

Elkanah's mother, Sarah was the daughter and fourth child of Samuel and Elizabeth Martin. The Martin family, along with the Davis family, led the group at Colerain which broke away and formed the Free Presbyterian Church.[9]

The Free Presbyterian Church Synod of the United States included former members of both Old School and New School Presbyterian churches who first withdrew and organized in Cincinnati in 1847.[10]

The "founder" was the Rev. John Rankin, a New School pastor in Ripley, Ohio. He had petitioned his denomination to exclude slaveholders from membership, which petition was rejected by the General Assembly. He and his congregation withdrew. Eventually more than 70 congregations joined them, in seven presbyteries, including 70 ministers and licentiates. Most of their congregations were in southern Ohio and western Pennsylvania. The church launched a newspaper, the *Free Presbyterian* in 1850 and founded Iberia College in 1854. [11]

> At the Colerain Presbyterian Church the pastor of the church, along in the latter forties or early fifties, had taken the position that the General Assembly of the Presbyterian Church was justified in its declaration that the ownership of slaves constituted no sufficient bar to Christian communion and fellowship in the Church. From this position some of its members, of strong character and conviction, led by James Martin and Abner Davis, Sr., withdrew from its membership and erected a church of their own near Andrew's Bridge,

---

[9] Marty Greenleaf, contemporary historian of Union Church. March history note online, 2016 being the 200th anniversary of this church.
[10] Andrew E. Murray, *Presbyterians and the Negro: A History*. Philadelphia: Presbyterian Historical Society, 1966, p.120. Presbyterian Historical Society.
[11] "John Rankin, Antislavery Prophet, and the Free Presbyterian Church," Larry G. Willey, *American Presbyterians*, 72:3 (Fall 1994), 165.

known as the Free Presbyterian Church, where there was maintained a separate minister, and service held until after the ratification of the Thirteenth Amendment.[12]

The strength of conviction of some Free Presbyterians leaders is reflected in this account:

> Rev. W. F. P. Noble, of Sadsbury township, a young Presbyterian minister, a scholar, and afterwards the author of two very readable books on religious topics, withdrew for a considerable time from the ministry, feeling that his conscience would not allow him to be as subservient to the institution of slavery as his congregation and the general church of the land expected him to be - especially after the weak position the church assumed in denouncing the Lovejoy outrage, in which the victim, a Presbyterian minister, was killed by a pro-slavery mob in Alton, Ill, in 1837, for having opposed slavery in a very mild and constitutional way in his paper. [13]

Although the Free Presbyterians started their own Iberian College, which admitted students of all races, they did not start their own missions board, rather they worked as an auxiliary to the American Missionary Association, from which they received some funding for their fairly poor congregations.

In addition to the *Free Presbyterian*, they also published the *Christian Leader*, and *Free Church Portfolio.* Some members were also involved with the Underground Railroad. In 1860, an Ohio crowd prevented the extradition of a fugitive slave, and thus the leaders were

---

[12] "The Early Abolitionists of Lancaster County" by Thomas Whitson, Esq., in *Historical Papers and Addresses of the Lancaster County Historical Society, Volume 15* Lancaster County Historical Society, 1911, pp75-76.
[13] ibid "The Early Abolitionists of Lancaster County"

jailed, including Rev. George Gordon, president of Iberia College. It is said incarceration hastened his death.

Their membership standards were most universally uncompromising in regard to slavery. They stated that the Scriptures, God's revealed will, were clearly opposed to slavery and the fugitive slave laws. They held that "no person holding slaves, or advocating the rightfulness of slaveholding, can be a member of this body. " And they applied this not only to exclude slave-holders, but to disassociate themselves from members of churches with slave-holders in them.

The Free Presbyterians were also strong supporters of antislavery political parties. Furthermore they would not associate with churchmen who voted for slavery-tolerant politicians.

They used their publications to expose the horrors of slavery, but particularly focused on the hypocrisy of the Presbyterian groups they had left. They rebuked the Old School Presbyterians for their growing popularity among slave-owners after the 1845 General Assembly at which it was concluded slave-ownership was not ground for expulsion. They scorned the New School camp for denouncing slavery at the same time as refusing to discipline/expel slave owners. In both cases they proclaimed that the highest priority of these other Presbyterians was not God's standards for holiness, but rather maintaining large membership rolls.[14]

Although respectful of each other's stand on abolition, the followers of William Lloyd Garrison and the Free Presbyterians were rivals for the allegiance of those who opposed slavery. The Garrisonians down-played Christian doctrine, and stated that the Free Presbyterian

---

[14] John R. McKivigan, *The War Against Pro-slavery Religion: Abolitionism and the Northern Churches, 1830-1965* Ithaca MY: Cornell U Press, 1984 Chapter Five: "Abolitionist and the Comeouter Sects",

sectarianism was destructive of the cause. Garrisonian strength was in New England, where the Unitarians were important to their movement. Thus, on the other side, the Free Presbyterians maintained the Garrisonians were pulling people away from the Christ by their secularism.

The Free Presbyterians were thus most comfortable in anti-slavery activities carried out in tandem with other openly Christian abolitionists - such as tract distribution, publications, and conventions.

Elkanah Mackey and his brothers, then, grew up in the midst of a community and church where this issue was one of the shibboleths. That James Love Mackey chose to go to Africa as a missionary and that he was zealous to raise up African church leaders had foundations in his upbringing amidst family and church.

Three brothers aspired to the Presbyterian ministry, which office was exacting in its requirements. Candidates had to be "taken under care" of a regional presbytery, trained and tested in Greek, Latin, Arts and Sciences, Theology, and Church History, as well as the doctrines of Church Government, and the Sacraments. In most cases the knowledge necessary to pass these examinations was acquired by attending a good academy or college, and then Princeton Seminary. Each candidate had to preach before his presbytery in order to be "sustained," "licensed," and finally, "ordained." The three [15] Mackey brothers worked toward their ordinations under the care of the Presbytery of Baltimore, then the new Presbytery of New Castle.[16]

Elkanah graduated from the College of New Jersey (Princeton) in 1852, receiving "first honours of his class"

---

[15] That there was also a fourth brother we will learn later in the story.

[16] *Record, Presbytery of New Castle,* vol. 8, 1845-64 (hereafter Record, New Castle)

then went on to Princeton Seminary.[17] As of July, 1853, he was tutoring incoming students.

Elkanah mentioned his tutoring in the course of the first one of his letters extent, the main burden of which is to forward a request from his brother James in Corisco, Africa [18], for tombstones, which are to be placed on the grave of his (first) wife, Elizabeth. She had died in Gaboon, very soon after they arrived in Africa. Within a year (some say a month) of her death, both Mr. and Mrs. Simpson, who had accompanied them, also died -- by drowning.[19]

Princeton July 18th 1853

Rev. J. C. Lowrie [20]

Dear Sir. I have received letters from my brother at Corisco requesting me to go on to N. York to attend to some matters for him. The only thing which need be attended to immediately is to get tombstones for Elizabeth's grave. He would like to have them ready to send by the return of the *Lowden* or *Gem*. When will they probably sail? In which will Bros William & Clemens go? I cannot very well go on to N.Y. until College opens, which will be in about 3 weeks, as I have two young men under my tuition who intend to enter. If I could get you to take the trouble of speaking for the stones I can attend to the other matters when I go on as I suppose neither of the vessels will sail within three weeks.

I will give you the description he sends me of them. He says "I want them of the following size and pattern. The head stone to stand above the ground 18 inches, to be about 5 inches thick and about 15 inches wide. And to be marked right on the top *Mrs. E. J. Mackey* and on the front side 1850. The foot stone to be made to correspond, smaller proportionably, and to

---

[17] P.H. Almanac, '59-60, p. 74

[18] Corisco is an island of Gabon (then Gaboon), West Africa

[19] P. H. Almanac, '68, pp. 119-127

[20] "J. C. Lowrie" may be a mistake for "W." or Walter Lowrie.

have on the top of it *E.J.M.* That is all I want marked on either.

"I suppose you can understand from this description exactly what I mean, but lest it might be obscure I make the following drawing of the head stone."[picture of headstone included with note: "The corners may be dressed above as you see fit to order. The cost will I suppose not be more than 10 or 15 dollars but I do not know. I would be glad to have them come by Capt. Lawlin."

Will you be so kind as to drop me a note as to the probable time at which the *Gem* or *Lowden* will sail & c.

Very Truly yours & c.

E. D. Mackey[21]

(side note indicates the letter was received July 20)

Thus Elkanah's earliest direct involvement with foreign missions was one in which the mortality of the missionary wife was very much at the forefront.

Nearly two years later, April 10, 1855, Elkanah was licensed by presbytery. He was assigned to work under the financial support of the Committee on Domestic Missions in the "home field" embracing Doe Run Village, Chatham, Unionville, and Kennett Square, [22] in Chester County, Pennsylvania. His brother James, home from Africa, was one of the ministers present at the meeting where Elkanah was licensed. At an October meeting,

---

[21] E. D. Mackey, LTR, to Rev. J.C. Lowrie, July 18, 1853, courtesy Presbyterian Historical Society, Philadelphia

[22] In the 20th century, the Kennett Square has become known as the commercial "mushroom capital of the world."

Elkanah reported he had been employed during the last six months "preaching in the missionary field assigned him by the Presbytery." His brother James returned to West Africa within several months.[23]

Some time during 1855-6 another Pennsylvania Presbyterian communicated with the New York Agency of the Western Foreign Missionary Society, concerning another mission field. Alexander Culbertson, who by then had been an important figure in the American Fur Company's operations for more than twenty years, wrote asking that a Presbyterian mission be sent to his wife's people, the Blackfoot Indians. The Blackfoot, who hunted the prairies of what are now Alberta and Montana, are a confederacy of three related tribes: the Blackfoot (*Siksika*), Piegan (*Pikani*) and Blood (*Kainah*) tribes. They were a major power on the northwestern Great Plains. [24]

> The attention of the Executive Committee was specially called to the claims of these Indians by Alexander Culbertson, Esq., who has resided for some time among them as agent of the American Fur Company; and who felt a sincere desire to see them brought under the influence of Christian civilization.[25]

The *Minutes and Reports* of that annual Presbyterian meeting of 1856 made this brief mention of the nascent Blackfoot Mission:

---

[23] Record, New Castle

[24] In addition to the Piegans or *Pikani*, the Bloods or *Kainah*, and the Blackfoot proper or *Siksika*, the Blackfoot confederacy also included the Gros Ventres who through many years were their allies, though not closely related.

[25] *General Assembly, 1857, Minutes and Reports*, Presbyterian Church in the USA, "Foreign Mission Reports," p.26. (hereafter GA 1857 Minutes and Reports, PCUSA)

> Besides the laborers whose names are reported above, the Rev. Nestor A. Staicos, of the Presbytery of Alleghany city, and is wife, and the Rev. Elkanah D. Mackey, of the Presbytery of Newcastle, and his wife, have been appointed as missionaries to the Board – the former to the Greeks, and the latter to the Blackfeet [26] Indians. They are expected to proceed to their respective fields of labor in May; but as the arrangements for these missions are but of recent date, and are not yet complete, a full account of them is reserved for the report of next year. [27]

We see that Elkanah has acquired a wife. The date of this happy event was 28th Feb 1856. The place, Rock Presbyterian Church, Cecil County, Maryland. The extensive denominational newspaper, *The Presbyterian*, March 15th issue, included this in its "MARRIED" column:

> On Thursday, the 28th ult., by Rev. Abraham De Witt, [28] E. D. MACKEY of Chester county, Pennsylvania to Miss SARAH E. ARMSTRONG of Cecil county, Maryland.[29]

---

[26] NOTE: Two plurals are used in reference to the people of the Blackfoot tribe or confederacy in this book. "Blackfeet" was commonly used by the missionaries and traders, as it is commonly used today by tribal members and others. However, since English usage is generally agreed that the plural of a proper name is not formed by internal vowel change, I have kept to "Blackfoots" where not quoting others.

[27] GA 1856 Minute and Reports, PCUSA, p.27

[28] Rock Presbyterian Church, Cecil Co., Maryland, seems to have been Sarah Armstrong's home church.

Abraham De Witt was pastor of Rock Presbyterian from 1841 to 1855, and continued to reside in Fair Hill, MD, after his retirement. *Necrological Reports of Princeton Seminary, 1888*, vol 1, pp 13-14 and *Biographical Catalogue of Princeton Theological Seminary, 1815-1932*, p. 58.

[29] *The Presbyterian*, March 15, 1856.

Well might the 1856 Report on the Blackfoot Mission be a bit vague. Whereas Elkanah and Sarah were certainly pledged and planning to go as missionaries to Native Americans, the Blackfoot tribe had not been among the "fields" in the Foreign Board's plans that year. Walter Lowrie, in a letter dated March 19, wrote, "Rev. E. D. Mackey & his wife will be ready in May or June. If there were a cabin for them, they would go at once to the Ottoes." [30]

Walter Lowrie, Secretary, Foreign Missions Board

---

[30] Walter Lowrie, LTR to ________, March 19, 1856.

The mission to the Otoes had been carried on by Moses Merril since about 1832. He published an Otoe hymnbook – "Hist. Recollections in and about Otoe County", *Neb. State Hist. Soc. 1* (1885) pp.45-6. –Was the board sending the younger Mackeys to replace him?

Walter Lowrie, Secretary to the Foreign Board, was one of those men whose energy and accomplishments seem beyond normal proportions. He served as a Pennsylvania Representative in 1811, and then for six years as a Pennsylvania Senator. He then served in the US Senate for a full term beginning in 1818.[31] He served on a number of standing committees, including those of Public Lands and of Indian Affairs. He was elected Secretary of the Senate on December 25, 1825, after which he lived in Washington and Butler, PA. After his wife died in November 1832, he continued in this Senate office until 1836.

His biographers point out that he held his secretariat during a very dramatic period:

> His eleven years in that post coincided with two periods that future historians dubbed the "Golden Age of the Senate" and the "Era of Andrew Jackson." The Senate's Golden Age began in the 1820s and continued for at least three more decades. As the slavery issue intensified, the Senate, with its equal number of slave states and free states, became the principal battleground for contesting that issue. From the 1820s until the Civil War, when new states entered the Union, they were admitted in slave-state, free-state pairs so as not to disturb that balance.
>
> In the five years between 1827 and 1832, the North, the South, and the West acquired articulate new Senate voices with the arrival of Daniel Webster, John C. Calhoun, and Henry Clay. These three men -- the Senate's "Great Triumvirate" -- helped elevate the Senate's popular image from that of a quiet debating society to a dynamic legislative forum.

---

[31] While in the Senate he said of the Missouri Compromise, "If the alternative be this: either dissolution of the Union, or the extension of slavery over the whole western country, I for one will choose the former."

The resulting political turbulence over slavery soon brought a new alignment of political parties. Although Andrew Jackson won the greatest number of popular and electoral votes in the 1824 presidential election contest, none of that race's four active candidates gained an Electoral College majority. Subsequently, the House of Representatives awarded the victory to John Quincy Adams, who had run second to Jackson in both popular and electoral votes.

Jackson's campaign to gain the presidency in 1828 dominated political debate for the next four years. In the 1828 rematch, he defeated Adams and began an eight-year administration that profoundly reshaped American political life. For the entire period of Walter Lowrie's secretaryship, fierce struggles between the Jacksonians and the Henry Clay-led opposition resounded through the Senate chamber and across the nation. [32]

Lowrie seems to have been an outspoken abolitionist, and it is said:

> His speech before the U.S. Senate protesting slave labor and the Missouri Compromise invoked a groundswell of support among colleagues against the extension of human bondage. [33]

He had been an active churchman, so it seems it was with a sense of calling that he resigned from the Senate turmoil, and became Secretary for the Western Foreign Mission Society of the Presbyterian Board of Foreign Missions. His involvement in missions was thereafter as extensive as possible.

---

[32] US Senate Art and History – www.senate.gov/artandhistory/history/ . . .

[33] "Walter Lowrie" http://www.legis.state.pa.us/cfdocs/legis/BiosHistory/ . . .

Although he did not die a martyr's death for the cause of Christian gospel, two or three of his eight children did. Two served in the China Missions field, in which Michael Simpson Culbertson, half-brother of Alexander, also served (and lost loved ones) in the cause. Walter M. Lowrie (jr.) was to be drowned by pirates in China, in 1847, and Reuben, who replaced Michael Culbertson in 1857, also died there in 1860. A third son, John Cameron lived long enough at least to write his father's *Memoirs*.[34] Jack Holterman's *King of the High Missouri* gives a great deal of information about the inter-connections between the Lowries and Culbertsons in the China field, and in the stateside Foreign Board.

In late 1855 or early 1856, Alexander Culbertson communicated with Walter Lowrie about a Blackfoot Mission. This seems to be the original impetus which set things in motion at the Foreign Board. We do not know how Culbertson's proposal was delivered. Jack Holterman suggests he may have traveled to New York and spoken personally with Lowrie.[35] More likely they met in Washington, D.C. We know a number of things about the proposal because we have Lowrie's reply:

> If we can get our missionaries ready we wish by all means they should go with you, If you go in May we think we can be ready, but it would suit us better to go in June. I hope you will get the contract for the govt. freight. Will you please to give us the earliest notice of the time you will set out.
>
> Also state what the expense of a passage will be from St. Louis to your establishment as nearly as you can. Will you please also state the kind and amount of

---

[34] Jack Holterman, *King of the High Missouri*, Ch. XI p. 71. indicates John Cameron Lowrie apparently also died in the India mission field. See also previous footnote.

[35] Jack Holterman, *King of the High Missouri*, Ch. XVIII, p. 123

supplies it will be proper for them to take with them, as flour, groceries, bedding, clothing, articles of house keeping, medicine (&c.)

What kind of funds should they take, gold or bank notes? Could they sell drafts on our treasurer payable (here?) ?

Have you decided on building a small steamer to run above Fort Union? Is so we will if you desire it advance you one thousand dollars which you can repay in freight and for assisting our missionaries in their building, and in labor & supplies as far as you have supplies which they may want. Please also state where letters (can?) reach you till you set out.

Answers to these questions will give you some trouble but they will greatly oblige us.

I am Dear Sir, Yours sincerely, Walter Lowrie [36]

The "govt. freight" and "a small steamer to run above Fort Union" seem to be matters Culbertson has mentioned in his earlier communications. The first has to do with the "Stevens Treaty of 1855," i.e. the previous year, which promised annuities to the Indians of the Northwest Plains, to be regularly shipped to the Upper Missouri. The American Fur Company expected to get the contract to haul these annuities upriver, but had competition from "the opposition" under Alexander Campbell.

The "small steamer" seems to refer to a new "mountain boat" as the Upper Missouri steamboats came to be called. Apparently Culbertson had mentioned or hinted at the possibility the mission could invest with the American Fur Company toward a better means of navigation for the highest (and most troublesome) stretch of river adjacent to the proposed mission field. The idea of

---

[36] Walter Lowrie, LTR to Alexander Culbertson, March 28, 1856

a small steamer had already been proposed to the govt. in connection with Indian Affairs.

However, the Upper Missouri was not yet even "navigable" insofar as any regular steamboat travel - and even in its heyday some thirty years later, it would often prove but barely navigable.[37]

Walter Lowrie had one pair of young missionaries on tap - originally planning to send them to another Indian mission as per this letter dated Mar 19, 1856, to Mr. Irvine, missionary to the Ottoes:

> . . .Rev. E.D. Mackey & his wife will be ready in May or June. If there were a cabin for them they would go at once to the Ottoes. I feel sorry to press you with so much business . . .[38]

We think Alexander Culbertson's proposal came rather suddenly at this time because he knew some of the clauses of the Stevens Treaty might provide incentives for a Presbyterian Mission. Lowrie mentions what this treaty promised in another letter to Seth Irvine nine days later, written the same day he replied to Culbertson:

> Mr. Mackey who was appointed to the Ottoes, is one of our best men & just the man for an Indian mission. But the providence of God is opening up new fields for our (other?) Indian mission (so?) that we hardly know what is duty -
>
> A treaty has been made with the Blackfeet, by which they receive $50,000 a year for 10 years. Of this $20,000 in goods, $15,000 for farming (equipment?), and

[37] The first steamboats that got all the way up the river to Fort Benton arrived in 1860. These were the Chippewa and the Far West II. Alexander Culbertson was among the passengers on that first trip.
[38] Walter Lowrie Letter to Seth Irvine, dated Mar 19, 1856, Presbyterian Historical Society

$15,000 for education. Father Smet [39] has already applied to take charge of the school funds

Group of Piegan Indians, From a painting by John Mix Stanley

. At Washington I learned that before the treaty is ratified, and the appropriations made, it would be too late to send the supplies this coming summer. When I reported these facts to the committee, they decided to send one or two missionaries & their wives this spring. But we have no more at present but Mr. Mackey. This morning we got permission of the Department to send the missionaries thence (?) & we have sent to Mr.

[39] Father Pierre Jean De Smet, S. J., one of the most respected early Catholic missionaries in Montana and the Northwest. That both the Catholics and the Presbyterians applied for this government money shows that "separation of church and state" in matters of education, etc., was not a concern at this time. Indeed ten years later, President Grant's "Peace Policy" in regard to Indian relations confirmed that the federal government was not Constitutionally or traditionally concerned to disassociate religion from its policies and spending.

> Mackey to come and see us. If he agrees to go, then we must look out for a man for the Ottoes. ...
>
> Please keep this account about the Blackfeet to yourself. De Smet talks of going up this summer, & we do not wish that he should know our purposes. If Mr. Mackey goes to the Ottoes, he will join you about the 1st May (?). Next week we shall know & will write. . . .

Lowrie also seems to be up-to-date in his knowledge of the plans of Father De Smet -- that somewhat more experienced, rival missionary, whose decision-making involved none of the complications of a wife. Lowrie was well-connected in the circles of the U. S. Senate and other offices of government. He had many friends in Washington including at least one president[40]. No doubt he employed these connections to stand the mission in good stead. Indeed, at least formally, some favor was shown the Presbyterian Blackfoot Mission:

> Department of the Interior
> Office Indian Affairs,
> March 27, 1856
>
> To the Superintendent of,and Agents within the Central Superintendency.
>
> Gentlemen.
>
> Understand that the Board of Foreign Missions of the Presbyterian Church will send out, during the coming Summer, to the country of the Blackfoot Indians a few Missionaries, who will be accompanied by their wives, you are requested to afford them all facilities and information, in your power, as may tend to promote success in their charitable aims.
>
> Very respectfully, Your Obt. Servt.
> Charles E. Mix, Acting Commissioner[41]

---

[40] John Cameron Lowrie, *Memoirs of the Hon Walter Lowrie*.

[41] In Guy S. Klett, "Missionary Endeavors of the Presbyterian Church Among the Blackfeet Indians in the 1850's," *Journal of the Department of*

Alexander Culbertson from a portrait by John James Audubon and Isaac Sprague

---

History, Presbyterian Historical Society, (PCUSA) vol XIX, Dec 1941 (no. 8) (hereafter, "Klett 'Missionary Endeavors' ")

CHAPTER TWO - Particular Call

In April Walter Lowrie wrote to another missionary:

> Mr. Mackey & his wife have been to see us, and they have agreed to go to the Blackfeet. If we can get another family to go with them we shall send them. It is a (pretty) serious matter for a lady to go to that (mission/region) unless another lady can be got to go with them. It will normally be but once a year that they can hear from home or write home.
>
> I would have been off next week, if it had not been for this mission. Now I will be delayed for two or three weeks. . . .[42]

Walter Lowrie

Since Alexander Culbertson knew Father De Smet well, and seems at one point to have asked him to arrange the baptism of his wife and their re-marriage[43], it might seem likely that it was from Culbertson that Lowrie learned of Father De Smet's application and intentions. But Lowrie indicates his news came from other sources:

> Mr. Mackey, who was appointed to the Ottoes has had his field changed and is now going to the Blackfeet. A

---

[42] Walter Lowrie, LTR , to Seth Irvine, April 4, 1856. Mr. Irvine had gone to the Iowa Indian mission with William Hamilton in the 1840s.
[43] Holterman, *King of the High Missouri*, p. 131

> treaty was made with them last summer, most liberal in its terms. For education the sum of $15,0000 a year for ten years, has been put in the treaty. I went to Washington in reference to this matter, but the Indian Office told me, it would not be able to carry out the treaty this coming summer, because it would be too late before the treaty could be ratified, & the appropriations made. I was also told that the Jesuits had made application to take charge of the education funds. When I reported the state of facts to the Committee on my return, they decided to send one or two missionaries and their wives, this summer, at the expense of the Board alone. Hence (?) we consulted Mr. & Mrs. Mackey, and they have agreed to go, themselves, if another family cannot be (?got). This appointment to the Blackfeet, we do not wish spoken of publicly, till our missionaries are (?already) starting, as it is something to get the start in a mission as important as this is.[44]

The Foreign Board was taking the Blackfoot Mission very seriously and moving with a haste rare for them (or for today's Presbyterian missions). Furthermore, they were funding the effort from their own budget, without support from individuals, congregations, and presbyteries. However they were counting on this bread cast upon the Muddy Missouri to return quickly, if not quite in the form it did return.

We might say then, that at the outset what launched the Mackeys up the Missouri to Montana in 1856 were four salient factors:

1/ An awakening zeal for the lost of foreign lands and tribes, and particularly for the American Indians.

2/ A suggestion by Alexander Culbertson that the time was right for a Blackfoot mission, especially because:

---

[44] Walter Lowrie, LTR, to Rev. W. H. (?Hannell/Hamilton), April 7, 1856

3/ A Treaty had just been made (1855) which allocated $15,000 for Blackfoot education, a thing dear to most missionary's' hearts, again especially when:

4/The Jesuits, in the person of Father De Smet, were applying for these same funds.

Father De Smet, Roman Catholic Indian missionary

Jack Holterman, author of an authoritative account of Alexander Culbertson's life, *King of the High Missouri,* (parts of which he kindly let this author see in pre-publication drafts) suggested the possibility the original idea for a Blackfoot mission came from Michael Simpson

Culbertson, who had been involved in China missions for about 12 years.[45] It is possible Michael had encouraged Alexander to pursue the idea, but as Lowrie's letters make clear, the Blackfoot mission received much of its impetus from the terms of the 1855 Stevens Treaty.

It was Alexander, considering what good might come of it to himself and American Fur, who also saw some good that might come of it for his wife's people and his denomination of origin. He had apprised Lowrie of the Treaty's provisions and thus the potential funding for a Presbyterian mission school. He must have genuinely expected some benefit to his wife's people - perhaps chiefly educational benefit.

Apparently as willing to outfit the Blackfoot mission as the outreach to the Ottoes, the Presbytery of New Castle prepared on April 8, 1856 to furnish their new and honored graduate of Princeton Seminary to that mission:

> The Presbytery having in view the ordination of Mr. Elkanah D. Mackey, licentiate, who expects, under appointment of the Board of Foreign Mission soon to set out to establish a new mission to the Blackfeet Indians, it was ordered that Mr. Mackey preach his trial sermon for ordination from Psalm 35:1, tomorrow at 4 o'clock P. M., and that the ordination services be conducted, if the way is clear, at 7 ¼ o'clock P. M.[46]

The way indeed appeared clear:

> After recess, the Presbytery proceeded, by prayer and the imposition of hands, to ordain to the work of the Gospel ministry, as an Evangelist, Mr. Elkanah D.

---

45 Holterman, Jack, Xerox copy of MSS chapter for *King of the High Missouri*, CH XVI, "Locust Grove"

46 Record, New Castle Presbytery, Vol 8, 1845-1864.

> Mackey, a licentiate of this Body. In the ordination service the Moderator [47] presided and proposed the Constitutional questions, Dr. Burrowes preached the ordination sermon from 2 Corinthians 3:18,[48] and Mr. Wynkoop delivered the charge to the Evangelist. Having by this act become a member of the Presbytery, his name was added to the roll.
>
> The stated clerk was directed to forward to the Boards of the Foreign Missions a notice of the ordination of Mr. E. D. Mackey, And of our recommendation of him as possessing suitable qualifications for the work of Foreign Missions. [49]

At the same meeting, Elkanah's younger brother, William D. "from the church at New London [PA]" was taken under care as a student on probation and recommended for Princeton Seminary under the Board of Education. [50]

Oldest brother James L. wrote the presbytery from West Africa and instructed them that a church had been organized at Corisco (Crisco in some references), which church should be entered on the presbytery lists. [51] Apparently new churches planted by foreign missionaries were joined to the US presbyteries from which the founding missionaries came. James had completed a grammar of the Benga language which was published in New York in 1855.[52]

---

[47] The moderator was Mr. Love. Note that the older brother, James Mackey's middle name was Love.

[48] "But we all, with open face beholding as in a glass the glory of the Lord, are changed into the same image from glory to glory, even as by the Spirit of the Lord." (II Corinthians 3:18)

[49] ibid.

[50] ibid.

[51] ibid.

[52] *One Hundred Years of Service By the Foreign Missionaries of Carlisle Presbytery, 1837-1937.*

Elkanah wrote to Walter Lowrie on the day of his ordination showing some of the progress of the Blackfoot mission:

> Walter Lowrie, Esq. Dover, Del, Ap. 8, 1856
>
> Dear sir, We reached home late on Sat. & were obliged to leave home before daylight yesterday in order to come to Presbytery. This is the best excuse I have to render for neglecting to write to you so long.
>
> Mr. Stewart thinks he could not possibly get ready to go with us to the Blackfeet. He has promised however to hold the matter under consideration with a view to going in the Fall, but seems to have his mind fixed on S. America.
>
> Can you put me in communication with Mr. Culbertson? What is his first name & his address?
>
> Will you send us a list of the articles you intend to purchase for the Blackfeet?
>
> We hope you will be able to get a family to accompany us.
>
> Yours truly & c. E. D. Mackey [53]

(A note on the letter says "Direct to New London, Pa.")

Apparently Elkanah succeeded in getting in touch with Alexander Culbertson, for they were soon to meet.

No other Blackfoot missionaries arose to the occasion, however, except Sarah E. Armstrong, Elkanah's betrothed, whose honeymoon was to be the journey west:

> In 1856 he was ordained as a missionary to the American Indians in Nebraska Territory; previous to leaving, he married Sarah E. Armstrong of Cecil Co., Md. [54]

---

[53] E. D. Mackey, LTR to Walter Lowrie, April 8, 1856

[54] Presbyterian Historical Almanac and Annual Remembrancer of the Church, Volume 2, for 1859-1860.

Alexander Culbertson from 1855 sketch by Rudolph Friederich Kurz

How Elkanah and Sarah met or when they became engaged we can but surmise. It appears they grew up in the same rural community, in congregations about ten miles apart, although in separate states -- Elkanah in Pennsylvania and Sarah in Maryland. The Presbytery of New Castle consisted of congregations from three states, including also Delaware.[55] Likewise congregations might draw from two or more states. The congregation in which they were married, Rock Presbyterian Church, of Cecil County, MD, had two graveyards associated with it as of the 1870s: one in Lewisville, PA, and one in Fair Hill, MD. Headstones in those cemeteries include fifteen inscribed with the family name of Armstrong and fourteen with that of Mackey. In 1872 that congregation included among its members five Armstrongs and eleven Mackeys. [56]

---

[55] Record, Presbytery of New Castle

[56] J. H. Johns, *A History of the Rock Presbyterian Church in Cecil Co.,*1872.

Among the Mackeys buried in the Pennsylvania graveyard was a William who died April 7, 1845, at the age of fifty-eight.[57] -- no doubt a relative, although his dates don't seem to be those of Elkanah's father.[58] A William Mackey lived "near the church" and was an elder. He is said to have been "a general in the militia of 1812."[59]

A Walter Armstrong is also listed as an elder of Rock Presbyterian, ordained on November 9, 1851.[60] Perhaps this was Sarah's father. Thus it is likely Elkanah and Sarah knew each other through the involvement of their families at least in the same presbytery. Their engagement seems likely to have taken place while he was at Princeton Seminary.

Elkanah and Sarah must have agreed on mission work among the Indians before they committed to marriage. In concert with the Foreign Board they first planned to go to the Ottoes (Nebraska). Together they went to New York to discuss the Board's newly expressed desire that they go to the Blackfoots, instead. They decided to do so with a few stipulations, or at least expressed particulars of what they would prefer.

Walter Lowrie wrote on April 21:

> I leave home on Monday the 28 and go direct to St. Louis. Mr. Mackey & his lady will meet me there & they expect to leave for the Blackfeet country on the 5th (?) May. After getting their purchases made I will ascend(?) at once to the Iowa mission. There I shall arrange with Mr. Irwin for the reception of yourself [Rev. W. H. Hannell] [61] and company, and when I have done what is

---

57 ibid.

58 Genealogical sources indicate Elkanah's parents were William Mackey (1783-1851) and Sarah Mackey (1790-1875).

59 ibid

60 ibid.

61 W. H. Hannell – an 1856 graduate of Danville Theological Seminary, Danville KY according to 1856 Presby. Gen. Assy. Reports

> wanted there I shall pass (?) on to Bellevue, and then any(?) other (?) missions. ...
>
> P. S. We have no missionary yet for the Ottoes, we shall be glad to hear from Mr. Young (?). We still need some one (?) in the fall and sooner if he can be obliging (?) W. L. [62]

Lowrie had considerable experience with missions, and out of that experience he attempted to inspire the new Blackfoot missionaries. He wrote and sent the following lengthy instructional letter to Elkanah, probably addressed to St. Louis:

> My Dear Sir May 7, 1856
>
> We have so little information of the people to whom in the providence of God you are sent to preach the everlasting gospel, that it is but five suggestions we can make for your instruction and guidance in the work before you. Mr. Culbertson, before you reach your field of labor, will be able to give you much information that will be of service to you, and we trust our blessed Lord, on whose service you go, will afford you grace and wisdom from on high, and make every path of duty plain before you.
>
> The first year must of necessity be one of preparatory work. This is more or less the case in every new mission, and one must not be surprised or discouraged to find it to be particularly so, in commencing a mission among a distant and savage people.
>
> With every disposition on the part of Mr. Culbertson, to make your accommodations comfortable, it may be they will be far inferior to what we would desire them to be. But if the Lord prospers the mission, this trial and inconvenience will be but temporary, and in the meantime you will make them as comfortable as

---

[62] Walter Lowrie, LTR, to ??, April 12, 1856

may be in your power at the expense of the Board. Bear in mind, that the winter will be long, and the weather cold, and provide in time for this state of things. The supplies sent with you are considered sufficient for eighteen months, except the article of meat, and for this you must get your supply at the Mission.

Consult with Mr. Culbertson as to the best mode of making your purchases from the Indians. They should receive a fair equivalent for everything you get from them, for it would only do injury to pay them too much, or too little, for any article, be it large or small.

If you can get a room in the Fort, or if you have more rooms than one to yourselves, the sooner you make the effort to open a school for the children, the better. [63] The number of pupils however should be small at first. Much patience, and perseverance, and kindness on your part will be required, in conducting the school. Experience must be your guide, for we have no Indian schools in all respects similar. You cannot speak to the children and they cannot speak to you. But if they attend regularly they will soon begin to understand what you wish them to do, and in the course of a year will learn a good deal of English.

You will confer with Mr. Culbertson as to what religious services in English can be conducted at the Fort. He & I were both so much engaged that this and other points were not mentioned. I would suppose that one sermon in English on the Sabbath might be conducted, at which all who chose might attend.

At our Indian missions, and also in Africa, India, and China, we have found a great advantage in teaching children music. In the Seminole school, small children sing the alphabet, and thereby learned the letters as an

---

[63] It's curious to see that Lowrie envisions the school opening as soon as possible - perhaps in the fort itself. I'm not aware of any fur company setting up a school on its posts' premises, but as Elkanah observes later, the mission might even have bought the place!

amusement. But the great advantage to them was in learning to sing in Psalmes and Hymns.

If you can get an Interpreter, you can make religious talks to the chiefs and all other Indians. In these you will of course at first communicate the truths of the Gospel in plain and simple language. Refer often to the bible as being God's book, given to the Indians as well as to the white man.

Mr. Culbertson will be able to fix the best time after your arrival, when you will explain to the chiefs the cause and motives of your coming among them. You will inform them that good men and women in the United States, have sent you to make known to them the truths of God's book. That this book tells of the true God, the great Spirit, who is the maker of the red man and the white man, and of all men in all parts of the world. That he made the sun and the moon and the stars &c &c. That you have come to teach their children also, so that they can know as much as the white man, read God's own book, read the books of the white man - work like the white man and in short be equal to the white man in all respects. Tell them also that your wife has come with you to instruct the Indian women and children.

Explain to them briefly that the good people of the churches have no less than 25 other missionaries, & 30 female teachers mostly their wives living among other tribes instructing the Indians that form the Choctaws, the Chickasaws, the Seminoles, the Creeks or Muskogees, the Iowas, the Sacs, the Omahas, the Chippewas, and the Ottawas, they have 500 Indian children in their schools, that many of these children and young men and young women have learned as much as the great mass of white people. They have all learned English, they can read and write, and in all respects can do what white men can do.

[Tell them] That Indian children can learn all these things, just as well as white children. That you did not come for the purposes of trade, or to make money but simply to do them good. That your expenses are paid by the good people who sent you, and that in all the churches, these good people pray for the blessing of God in the Indians, and especially on the Indian schools and children under the care of these missionaries. That if it is the wish of the chiefs and people, and your health should be spared you are willing to spend your life in doing them good, and when God's time comes, you are willing to die and be buried among them.[64] And if they desire it, other missionaries and teachers will be sent out to assist you. These and any thing else that Mr. Culbertson may suggest you can state to them.

A Buffalo Hunt, taken from a lithograph : "Blackfeet Indians - Three Buttes" by John Mix Stanley

In reference to the picture, we shall need information from you on several points, most of which you will be able to send by Mr. Culbertson on his return.

[64] This part of the Mackey's instructions is particularly poignant taken in hindsight.

1st. The manner you have been received by this people and your impressions respecting them.

You may not have time to go much into detail on these points, and first impressions are not always to be depended on even by those whose wish is to work simple unity. We shall like to know however how they receive you & especially how they receive Mrs. Mackey.

2. We shall want information in regard to a site for the Mission. This will be a question of some importance to decide, and perhaps cannot be decided on, till the plan of instruction if first decided. If the teaching be in a day school, then the site ought to be near enough to an Indian village, for the children to attend.

We have but little confidence however in the benefits to result from day schools and for some tribes they cannot be conducted to any advantage, and in some hunter tribes they cannot be conducted at all. When the children are clothed in skins, and live in the lodges of their parents, they are sometimes not in condition to be brought to school. How it is with the Blackfeet, I cannot say. Even when they can attend, they soon dislike the confinement of the school, and their attendance becomes irregular or is given up. We look therefore with much interest to the establishment of a boarding school.

This is an expensive establishment, and if carried on with the funds of the Board alone, will be far less extensive than the wants of the people require. But as a beginning has been made, the committee must look to the churches for the means to sustain it, even if supported by themselves. We will try I think to support a school of 40 or 50 children if the prospects are good among the people themselves. For a boarding school, the site of the mission should be three, or four , or five miles from any Indian village. It should be placed convenient to timber, and to land good for farming purposes.

We will need some estimate of the expense of the buildings, & the plan we can talk over when we meet at Bellevue. By using adobe brick, the walls can be put up & the partitions of the same, which will much lessen the expense. One important item will be to procure laborers, and at what price, also the expenses of boards and shingles. On all these you can consult with Mr. Culbertson, in reference to the building we may agree upon. If however the Department assign all the school funds to our direction, we shall want a building capable of containing 80 or 100 scholars. If the chiefs and people cordially give the measure of their support, and would send a portion of their children from each band, such a school with the blessing of God, would be as life from the dead to this entire people. The estimates you may send us for the smaller building, will be a guide for the large one, if it be the will of God that it come under our direction.

3. The article of clothing for the children will claim your attention. I am fearful, that nothing this people possess, will answer in this purpose. I do not see how you could get on with them clothed in skins. But it may be that some of their outer garments for the winter may be made of skins. Shoes is an expensive article, and I would suppose the children might all use mokasans in the winter. We can send suitable clothing for both summer & winter, if it be found to be indispensable.

4. The article of beds & bedding is also expensive. This also I would suppose can be supplied chiefly by the use of buffalo robes. But we can only draw attention to this matter, and wait for information from you.

5. The article of food for the children is also one of much importance. If the diet they have been accustomed to can be obtained for them, or for the principal part of their food, it will be a great matter. To support them with flour or corn meal sent from St. Louis, would be too expensive. Yet you may need a portion of these, and of bacon to use in part. In time we

can raise corn & perhaps hogs, & cattle to aid in the supply. This point also will require your particular attention.

6. Another important and difficult matter is female help for the kitchen, dining room, and work house. If thought advisable we may be able to send two of the young Indian women from the same mission [Iowa mission, see same paragraph.] But an important inquiry is can you get any assistance from the Blackfeet women? Unless this point can be answered satisfactorily, it will make the whole effort to establish a boarding school, large or small, a very doubtful measure. On this point consult with Mr. Culbertson, and give us all the information in your power. I may get some information respecting the young women, at the Iowa mission, before I see you at Bellevue.

7. The committee have no thought of leaving you at this mission alone. We won't have time to have such another brother and sister with you now, and will do so, to that extent at least the next spring. If the mission receive the support of the Department, they will enlarge accordingly.

8. You go, Dear brother and sister, to a new and untried field of labor. It cannot be but you will experience much inconvenience and discomfort till you get a house & buildings of your own. For the summer & the long winter you will be separated from all your former friends and faith and patience will be needed to sustain you in these circumstances of trial. But think of the precious souls of this perishing people.

Think often of him, who though he was rich for our sakes became poor - Think of the power of the Holy Spirit, to bless your labors, and to redeem and sanctify this down trodden and neglected people, & make them the children of the living God. They must have the agency of God's people, to tell of him who came to seek and to save the lost; and his truth as dispensed by you will not return unto him void. God has a people among them, and he will bless your labors, to bring them into the fold of Christ. You will not be forgotten by God's people, though you are far separated from them. Many prayers will go up to the throne of God in behalf of the Blackfeet Indians, and of his servants, who have gone to them with the bread of life.

With affectionate regard, I am yours,
Sincerely Walter Lowrie[65]

Among the facets of contemporary mission perspective illustrated in Lowrie's letter, most striking to this writer, and perhaps most relevant to the Mackey's decisions regarding their mission to the Blackfoots is the ambiguity illustrated in the last three sentences of the letter. "God has a people among them," meaning among the Blackfoots, but "You will not be forgotten by God's people, though you are afar separated from them," meaning your white friends back home. Perhaps Lowrie is a bit clumsy in stating what was put better later that year:

> Mr. and Mrs. Mackey will undoubtedly receive a hearty welcome, and in the course of time, with the blessing of God, have the honour and privilege of founding a Christian church among them. For the time being, they cannot but feel their isolation from the civilized world, and we earnestly bespeak for them the prayers of Gods people, that they may be sustained, and be permitted to realize their own and the hopes of the Christian Church in relation to these far off Indian tribes. This mission will be reinforced as soon as suitable persons can be found to take part in this good and great work [66]

Whether she kept one prior to this we do not know, but Sarah kept a diary for most of the trip to what is now Montana. We are indebted to her grandson, Wilmer

---

[65] Klett, "Missionary Endeavors".

[66] *The Home and Foreign Record,* Presbyterian Church in the USA, vol VII, 1856, September, p. 271 (hereafter "Home and Foreign Record")

Mackey Sanner for a published transcript of that diary. [67] The first entries read:

> *Monday, April 28th, 1856.* Left home to go to Fort Benton, [Benton] Nebraska [Territory], to establish a new Mission among the Blackfeet Indians. Brother Sammy and Wm. Mackey accompanied us to the depot, reached Philadelphia 1 o'clock, expected to get our business done to proceede on our jorney Tuesday morning, but not succeed.
>
> April 29th. Wrote a letter to Mother and one to Ma. E. wrote to Bro. Sammy, also added a postscript to my two. got Life insurence policy of $2,000. Minded to sending our boxes on to St. Louis, retired four o'clock P.M. slept till half past nine, got ready for eleven o'clock train.
>
> *April 30th.* On our way to St. Louis, got tickets to Pittsburgh by the Penna. Railroad, cars very full. E. could not get a seat by me till we reached Landcaster, a lady got out there. took breakfast at Altuna about ten o'clock, reached Pittsburgh 2 o'clock. Before proceeding farther on our jorney I must take a view of the smoky town, such a place I never looked at, it is a real black dirty smoky place, it did not take long to satisfy ether of us as we had no inclination to stay any longer than we could get away. We stood our journey so well we concluded to go on in the cars to Cincinnati, left between

---

[67] Wilmer Mackey Sanner, *The Mackey Family, 1729-1975,* copyright 1974. Although Wilmer corrected Sarah's spelling in his transcript, this author has gone back to her original creative spelling, which contrasts with her educated vocabulary. Spelling wasn't quite as important in those days as witness sayings of the day, such as President Jackson's: "It is a damn poor mind that can think of only one way to spell a word." The author is deeply indebted to Sarah's great-granddaughter and her great-great grandson for access to the original diary and permission to re-publish it. The copyright, of course, remains with the heirs of Wilmer Mackey Sanner.

4 & 5 with an other night's travel before us, a few miles out of Pittsburgh the cars stoped, a boy singing or rather hollowing around the cars, we looked out, there stood a poor boy with a cluster of fingers & toes on each hand & foot, I do not know how many, but they were short & thick so that they stood out, he comes to the cars every day to get money from the passengers.

May 1st. Reached Cincinnati about eight o'clock, went right down to the river, engaged our passage in the *Telegraph*, left about one o'clock, reached Louisville, Kentuckey that night, changed boats in the morning, got on *Alvan Adams*, [68] had a very pleasant trip to St. Louis, reached there May fourth Sab. night. Mr. Mackey preached on the boat Sab. morning, had a very attentive congregation. Some of the passengers expressed great gratification as they had not expected preaching.

[May 30th.] [69] I find in looking over my journal, that I have overlooked mentioning a very interesting family, who came on the boat with us from Cincinnati to St. Louis. After remaining there for several days, we were surprised & delighted to join them on the boat we took for Bellevue. We had the pleasure of their company as far as St. Joe, where they left us. In all there was eleven of them. Mr. & Mrs. Lovell, their four children, Mrs. Wilden, Mrs. Lovell's Mother, & Mr. Wildin, her son, his wife and one child & another gentleman that the children called Uncle Mosses. They were all very pleasant and we became much attached to them, the children were great company for us, they called us Aunt

---

[68] Occasionally . . . one comes upon such a vessel as the McKeesport-built *Alvin Adams* (592 tons, 1853) owned by eight men from seven different places, including Boston, Philadelphia, and Baltimore. The boat was named for Alvin Adams of Boston who held an eighth interest in her. – *Steamboats on Western Rivers*, footnote, p 359.

[69] This entry although the date is out of order, is placed here in our narrative since the events mentioned began at this point in the chronology, although she did not record them until later.

& Uncle. Mrs. Wilden's little Bell was a great little sufferer, but very patient. We were very sorry to part with them, felt lost without them.

May 5th. got off & put up at the Verginia Hotel in St. Louis, met Mr. Lowrie & Mr. Culbertson there, we remained there till wednesday.

Walter Lowrie, himself, had gone to St. Louis to attend to the Mackey's departure, as well as to other mission business:

> The decision of the Executive Committee to send a mission to the Blackfeet Indians made it necessary, also, that one of the officers of the Board should visit St. Louis, to arrange with the American Fur Company for the passage of the missionaries up the Missouri river, and to purchase and forward the necessary supplies.
>
> I reached St. Louis on the 1st of May, and the Rev. E. D. Mackey and his wife, for the Blackfeet Mission, arrived on the 5th. I was treated in the kindest manner by the senior and other partners of the American Fur Company, and the details of the arrangement were referred to Alexander Culbertson, Esq.
>
> This gentleman is a warm friend of missions to the Indians, and has more definite and extensive information in relation to the tribes of the upper Missouri than I had ever found before, either from books or individuals. He was going up in charge of the Company's boat, a steamer of two hundred tons[70], built expressly for the difficult navigation of the Missouri river.
>
> Mr. Culbertson gave me most valuable assistance in making out a list of supplies, and took much interest in Mr. and Mrs. Mackey, and extended to them every courtesy and encouragement. As it was uncertain when the Company's boat would leave St. Louis, it was

---

[70] The sidewheel steamboat *St. Mary,* Joseph La Barge, master.

> deemed best that Mr. Mackey and his wife should proceed to Bellevue, and remain with Mr. Hamilton's family, till Mr. Culbertson's boat should reach that point. [71]

The Mackey's left St. Louis in mid-May traveling as far as the Bellevue Mission on the *Edinburgh* ,[72] one of approximately 65 steamboats operating on the lower Missouri during 1856.

> *May 7th.* Took passage on the *Edenburg* for the Omaha Mission, made a mistake & went to Omaha instead of stoping at Bellevue where we reached on friday 16th, we were obliged to wait for the return of the boat as we could not get a private conveance on Sat. although it was only ten miles across the country, the boat remained there till Sab. morning the 18th, we reached Bellevue about half past eleven, A. M. Mr. Kinney who attends to fraight, had our trunks stowed away, then told us where Mr. Hamilton lived and insisted on us taking his buggy and he would walk up, of this I was very glad. It was very warm and I was not very well,[73] we came to the[re] and inquired of a lady (who proved to be Mrs. Hamilton) if that was where Mr. Hamilton lived. She answered us that it was, they knew we were coming, & were looking for us. Mr. Lowrie got there the day before. [17 May]
>
> We were late for meeting but as it was very neer we went & heard Mr. Hamilton preach the latter part of his sermon. Mr. Lowrie gave us a discorse in the

---

71 *Home and Foreign Record*, pp 239-41.

72 *Edinburgh*. Blount, master, was a Lightning line packet that operated on the Missouri from 1853 to 1859 – *Collections of the Kansas State Historical Society*, Volume 9, p. 301.

73 This is the first hint that Sarah was pregnant. Calculating back from the baby's birth, it seems she would have been about six weeks pregnant at this point. Had they known a few weeks earlier, it seems certain their plans would have been different.

> evening on the subject of Missions, it was exelent, he spoke an hour and a half and no one seemed to be weary. We have had a long wait for the boat. Mr. Hamilton's family consists of his wife & four daughters, all very pleasant & try to make us feel at home. We go to gather strawberries almost every day & have quite a feast for tea. Bellevue is situated on a high bluff, about half a mile from the Missouri River. It has the appearance of making a promising & flurishing town, there are not many buldings, at preasant, but is improving rapidly, they talk strongly of the railroad passing through there, the prosperity of the town depends much on that.

Although as unaware as most Americans of what was coming in five years, the Mackeys had good opportunity to hear the ominous rumblings of incipient Civil War as they traveled up the Missouri in 1856.

Congress had passed the Kansas-Nebraska Act on May 30, 1854, under the sponsorship of Stephen Douglas. It effectively repealed the Missouri Compromise of 1820, which prohibited slavery north of latitude 36°30´. Thus it allowed voters in the territories of Kansas and Nebraska to decide for themselves whether or not to allow slavery within their borders. This meant that pro-slavery and anti-slavery groups began to actively recruit settlers toward the goal of political domination in the polls that would determine the outcome. Considerable zeal for this project was generated in parts of New England and the South.

For example. on April 23, 1856, the steamboat *Keystone*, Thomas I. Goddin, master, left St. Louis carrying a party of southern emigrants headed for Kansas, under the leadership of Colonel Buford's. *Keystone* made sixteen trips on the lower Missouri that year. [74]

---

[74] Collections of Kansas State Historical Society, Vol 9.

But beyond the movement of genuine settlers, strong pro-slavery contingents in Missouri sent illegal voters to Kansas to help elect territorial representatives, and then even more (5000 or so) fraudulent voters to elect the territorial legislature, such that the results were 36 pro-slavery delegates and 3 anti-slavery delegates.

President Franklin Pierce had appointed a Pennsylvanian, Andrew Horatio Reeder, as Territorial Governor and he arrived in Kansas in October, 1854. Reeder was a Democrat sympathetic to the South and slavery. However his attitude changed after the March election when thousands of Missourians overran the polls in Kansas. The governor was shocked at the extent of the fraud and agreed with the Free Soil protests against the election. He discarded the results from all districts where protests were filed, and arranged for new elections in each of these. The new elections were boycotted by proslavery forces. The governor convened the legislature on July 2, 1855 in the new town of Pawnee, farther from the pro-slavery influences of Missouri.

Nonetheless, in this session of what came to be called "the Bogus Legislature" nearly all the members who were opponents of slavery were ousted. One anti-slavery legislator, John A. Wakefield, is said to have prophesied, "Gentlemen, this is a memorable day, and may become more so. Your acts will be the means of lighting the watch-fires of war in our land."

The seat of government was moved back to the Shawnee Methodist Mission near the Missouri border, despite Governor Reeder's veto, and the legislature reconvened there. This "legislature" then passed harsh laws against expressing anti-slavery opinions, and death sentences for those aiding escaped slaves. Voting laws were modified to allow non-residents (read Missourians) to vote - and the legislature made these retroactive to protect the fraudulent votes that elected them! They petitioned President Franklin Pierce for Reeder's removal, The president did fire the Kansas governor, citing his "private speculative interests," which charge seemed to have had some basis in Reeder's extensive land purchases.

Reeder remained in Kansas for a time, supporting the free-state movement, which independent of the legislature, "elected" Reeder and Jim Lane to the U.S. Senate in the event the Topeka Constitution should be recognized as Kansas was admitted to the Union -- which didn't happen. Reeder went down the river politicking

On May 5, the *David Tatum,* a large side-wheel boat brought Governor Reeder back up to the territory, taking only four days from St. Louis. But there a pro-slavery grand jury brought an indictment against him for high treason. As things heated, another Missouri river packet, *J. M. Converse*, arrived at Kansas City on May 21, 1856. Three days later, disguised as a woodhawk, Reeder made his escape on the *Converse* as it departed Kansas City. [75] He returned to practice law in Pennsylvania, and became active in Republican Party politics until he died in 1864. [76]

The pro-slavery elements did all they could to block anti-slavery efforts on the river.

In 1856, *The Star of the West* took a pro-slavery contingent up to the territories. This Missouri river packet, with William H. Parkinson, master, was a large side-wheel boat. She landed at Kansas City April 12, with 100 emigrants from Georgia, Alabama, South Carolina, and Kentucky. [77]

In late June the same year the same boat was featured in the following news article, which appeared in the *St. Louis Intelligencer*, citing as source the first Missouri river boat the Mackeys had traveled on:

---

[75] Collections of Kansas State Historical Society, vol 3, pp 205-223.

[76] Collections of Kansas State Historical Society, vol 9.

[77] Transactions of Kansas State Hist. Soc., Vol 9.

> The *Star of the West*, as we learn from the *Edinburgh*, is having trouble with her passengers. When the *Edinburgh* passed down the boat was lying at Weston [about 40 miles below St. Joseph] with the whole crowd on board, and with no prospect of landing them at any point. The passengers on board, it is known, are abolitionists, and, after having had their arms taken from them at Lexington [about 70 miles below Lawrence] the boat proceeded to Weston, but on her arrival there the inhabitants of the town and surrounding country refused to allow them to come on shore; and the only alternative now left is for the boat to bring them back and land them where she got them, which we learn will be done. [78]

Missouri-based pro-slavery groups may have been the most paranoid. According to a contemporary source, their fears focused in interesting places - such as a musical instrument transported by the *Genoa*, a packet that brought several persons in our story part way up the river in 1856. The Kansas Historical Society's archives contain a "letter of W. H. Russell, Lexington, Mo., to J. Riddlesbarger & Co, Kansas City, relative to a box on board the steamer *Genoa* containing a piano, supposed by Missourians to contain guns for Kansas, March 21, 1856."[79]

Things were indeed heating up. Many of the missions and the missionaries became anti-slavery bases, but just as many contemporary evangelical Christians are cool toward anti-abortion activists in their midst, most missionaries felt gospel preaching and education were their priorities. They were afraid they might lose their platforms for these things through abolitionist

---

[78] *St. Louis Intelligencer*, June 28, 1856

[79] Kansas State Historical Society, 8th biennual report, (for period 1890-92) p. 33.

associations. Therefore abolitionist activity was left to extremists like John Brown, who retaliated in ways as violent and ungodly as the pro-slavery forces.

Although Elkanah and Sarah followed Lowrie west and met him in St. Louis a few days after he arrived, he had sent them on alone to Bellevue, to wait at the Omaha Mission. Walter Lowrie's narrative of his own, separate travels continues:

> ...On Monday, the 2d of June, I left [the Sac Mission, having spent four weeks visiting the various mid-west missions] for St. Louis, and arrived there on Friday morning, the 6th. Found Mr. Culbertson still there but ready to leave. He had been detained in getting the government freight for the upper tribes.
>
> We left [on the way back east] on the 8th of June.
>
> There were more than one hundred men aboard the boat. Mrs. Mackey will be the only lady in so large a company. [80] The accommodations on board the boat were very good, and Mr. Culbertson told me his hands were all picked men, used to regulations and employment of the Fur Company.
>
> How much our missionaries need the prayers of the churches to enable them to sustain the various trials they meet in their Master's work!
>
> Mr. Culbertson reached Bellevue on the 22d[81] of June, where Mr. and Mrs. Mackey were received on board. [82]

Walter Lowrie seems to have joined the Mackeys for a few days earlier in the middle of his circuit around

---

[80] He was in error. There were several ladies in the Chouteau's party aboard *St. Mary,* and Mrs. Culbertson and her daughter, Fanny, were to join the Mackeys et al at Fort Pierre.

[81] Lowrie mixed his dates here. Sarah's Diary shows them boarding the *St. Mary* at Bellevue on 16 June. Elkanah's journal entry,1 July, says they left Bellevue on the 17th.

[82] *Home and Foreign Record*, pp 239-41

the missions. [Sarah's Diary indicates he arrived there 17 May] Elkanah mentions parting company with Walter Lowrie at Bellevue on the 27th of May, when he left for the Sac and Iowa Missions.[83] In the interim between parting from Lowrie, and embarking on the steamer up the river, Elkanah wrote his mission chief a letter about his plans and concerns:

> My Dear Sir,
>
> We are here yet in daily expectation of our boat. Mr. Childs starts this evening for the East & I embrace the opportunity of sending you a few lines.
>
> You recollect Mr. Jenkinson the mason, with whom you became acquainted here & who has gone up along the Blackbird. I have been thinking that it would be a very wise move to secure his services for Fort Benton next summer. I have spoken to him about going up, provided we conclude to build of concrete & should need his services. He will get a good deal of experience in that way this summer and appears to me to be a very reliable man. He says he would be perfectly willing to go to Fort Benton, if he should be needed, & knows no reason why he should not go as well as anyone else. His family consists of himself & wife, they have no children. If they could be induced to go and remain as missionaries they might afford a valuable assistance. I promised to write to him direct to Bellevue in care of Mr. Hamilton. If he goes up to Fort Benton he says he will take his wife along. -Sarah is well & unites with me in kind regards to you and Mrs. Lowrie.
>
> Truly and affectionately yours & c. E. D. Mackey [84]

The juxtaposition of the last two sentences in the letter was not pure happenstance. Elkanah was interested

---

[83] ibid.

[84] E. D. Mackey, LTR, to Walter Lowrie, June 4, 1856

in the builder, but was more interested in having a female companion and assistant for Sarah.

The practice in Presbyterian missions at the time was to send out teams consisting of at least two couples, and in some cases (as in the China mission during many years), four or five couples might go out together. The famous Oregon mission included Mrs. Whitman and Mrs. Spaulding, [85] with their husbands and a third man.

The second rule in Presbyterian missions, seems to have been: establish a school. Elkanah was operating under the instructions of the Board (expounded in the long letter from Lowrie, above) to determine the feasibility and particulars for building a school for Blackfoot children. The Jenkinsons sounded likely to fulfill the requirements of both rules. In his letter of September,'56, Lowrie seems to agree.

At Bellevue, the Mackeys had been enthusiastically welcomed by the other missionaries:

> Our stay at Bellevue was as pleasant as our friends there could make it. We were treated by Mr. Hamilton's family with the greatest kindness, and formed a strong attachment for them. It seemed like leaving home again when the St. Mary arrived, and we were summoned away.

The hospitality of the Hamiltons is attested by a number of sources:

> Rev. Mr. Hamilton was in charge of the Presbyterian Mission, and Mrs. Hamilton and the Misses Amanda, Maria, Elsie, and Mary Hamilton bore most prominent

---

[85]First two white women to cross the nation on the Oregon trail. Apparently they also crossed the southwest corner of present Montana, together with at least one other, precluding Sarah Mackey from being "the first white woman in Montana".

parts in the home and social life of that period. The mission house, in which they resided, was the one building of any size and degree of comfort for some time, and within its walls Father Hamilton received and Mrs. Hamilton entertained many and varied guests.[86]

Bellevue Mission from an engraving after Karl Bodmer, artist who accompanied naturalist Maximilian von Weid in 1832-34.

Despite the kindness of the Bellevue missionaries, its clear the Mackeys were champing at the bit:

> *June 16th.* Our stay in Bellevue has been prolonged four weeks & one day, twice as long as we expected to be there. But yonder comes a boat up the river lo! and Behold! it is the *St. Mary* at last, Here we are safely in the boat on the evening of the 16th. . . .

The Home and Foreign Record, a monthly magazine of the Presbyterian Church contained a three page article that

---

86 *Nebraska Women in 1855,* Harriet S. MacMurphy. Nebraska State Historical Society, 1897. p 164.

September, entitled "BLACKFEET INDIAN MISSION" which speaks both of the Mackey's journey and the people to whom they were going:

> . . .The steamboat left Bellevue, where Mr. and Mrs. Mackey were awaiting its arrival, on the 17th of June, and reached Fort Union, near the junction of the Yellow Stone and the Missouri, on the 10th of July.
>
> Mr. Mackey's journal is occupied with an account of the journey between these two points, and with some notices of the Indian tribes along the Missouri and cannot therefore fail to be interesting to the readers of the *Record*.
>
> The party were still five hundred miles distant from the place of their destination, four hundred of which would have to be traveled over land. [87]
>
> The Blackfeet Indians reside along the eastern base of the Rocky Mountains and not far from the two principal sources of the Missouri river. Their population is supposed to be fifteen thousand. They are represented by those who have been among them as mild and friendly in all their intercourse with white men, [88] but are held in fear by the less powerful Indian tribes in the same region of country. In many respects they are considered one of the most interesting and promising of all the Indian tribes of the Northwest, and, no doubt, important results may be expected from the mission about to be established for their good. [89]

---

[87] The calculations here are erroneously based on the Mackey's accounts which speak of the *St. Mary* going a hundred miles above Fort Union. The mistake lies in the fact that the boat traveled back to Fort Union before they set out on their overland journey – so that they went the full distance to Fort Benton by land.

[88] Although this description was fairly accurate for the decade in which it was written, it would have surprised those interlopers earlier and later, who experienced intense Blackfoot hostility.

[89] *Home and Foreign Record*, p. 271

Sarah's Diary records their excitement at getting aboard the *St. Mary* on the evening of the 16th:

> . . . They have tied the boat up for the night. Mr. Hamilton and his daughters accompanied us to the wharf. We were glad to proseede on our jorney, but very sorry to part with friends again.

Sarah was pleased to be on the way to Fort Benton, but also quite pleased with the *St. Mary* and its passengers:

> *June 17th.* The boat was off by the peep of day, we made head way rapidly today, went about a hundred miles, we have a very pleasant boat and the best of boarding, I like every thing about it, a great deal better than the *Edenburg* [*Edinburgh*] in which we came from St. Louis to Bellevue. We have also very pleasant passengers.
>
> Mr. Chauteau [Chouteau] (one of the Fur Company) and his family, consisting of his wife, four children, two servents girls & a elderly widow, whome they calle Mrs. McDonneld, they are all very pleasant.

Although they must have passed Omaha the morning they left Bellevue, Sarah does not mention it in her Diary. However, a number of sources [90] record that the *St. Mary*, in early June of that year, brought an incredible number of passengers to Omaha, 900 of them!

Note that the dates don't seem to be reconcilable to what we know of the Mackey's journey on *St. Mary*,

---

90 These sources include various lists of Missouri river boats, including several published in *Contributions to the Kansas Historical Society*, but the one furnishing most of the data used here is: "Riverboats of Capt. Joseph LaBarge " online, submitted by Matt Rowley, who notes, "This list is derived from *Way's Packet Directory* - 1848-1994.

nonetheless here is a contemporary account from the *Sioux City Eagle* of 4 June 1856 :

> We venture the assertion that the Railroad Packet *St. Mary* left for Omaha Saturday night [31 May] with the largest passenger list ever before crowded on any steamer on the Western Waters. She had 900 passengers aboard, 735 of whom were Mormons on the lower deck. But very few of the Mormons took cabin passage, probably less than 50, but the decks were one living mass of humanity. What a fearful responsibility rested on the pilot and the engineer! Just think! Nine hundred souls entrusted to their care. [91]

The 675 Mormons who did not take cabin passage were "deck passengers" and had to stake out their own sitting, standing, or sleeping space on the main deck somewhere.

It is true that Omaha was the Missouri River port through which many of the Mormon immigrants traveled that year on their way to Utah. This was partly because for those following a northern route, the Chicago and Rock Island Railway would take them as far west as Iowa City, and from there they could travel overland across through Des Moines to Omaha. Omaha was the starting point for the "Mormon Trail," three slightly divergent routes to the Salt Lake.

The Mormon "handcart companies" set out that year from Florence, just to the north of Omaha – but where were the passengers spoken of in the article coming from? One explanation is that they only took a short trip from the north side of the river across and up

---

[91] Item in *Sioux City Eagle,* June 4, 1856; cited under *St. Mary* in *Way's Packet Directory*, 1848-1994.

to Florence, now northern Omaha. Captain LaBarge and Charles Chouteau might have taken advantage of this unplanned opportunity for a short term profit. Even if the trip was only for several hours, the operation of taking 735 people aboard and stowing their baggage must have been something of an event. (We will say a little more about the Mormon handcart companies later where the Mackeys meet Jim Bridger.)

Other records refer to the *St. Mary* as a "railroad packet, " including a report of her demise in 1859, but the term is confusing, for the railroad to St. Joseph was not completed until 1859, and what, then was the "railroad" connection? "Packet" seems originally to have meant a conveyance chartered by government to carry mail, etc., but along the line the term came to refer to a vessel making regular trips between two points. Almost every steamboat fit one if not both of these descriptions.

If the *Sioux City Eagle* had its facts straight, and the point of embarkation was St. Louis, it may be the 735 Mormons left that city on 31 May (Saturday) and were still aboard when the Mackeys came aboard at Bellevue. . Yet it seems incredible they make no mention of it! And it is difficult to reconcile the dates, even if the Sioux City newspaper was quoting a St. Louis news item of a few weeks earlier.

My speculations leave me with three other possibilities: 1/that this happened another year [92] ;

---

[92] In support of this alternative I find this interesting assertion: "The *Sioux City Eagle* was the first paper published here. It was edited by Seth W. Swiggett, who died a few years ago in Chicago. In politics the *Eagle* was neutral with democratic leanings. Its first issue was put out on July 4th, 1857. (*Proceedings of the Academy of Science and Letters of Sioux City. Sioux City,* published by the Academy, 1904-1906. 2v.) underscore added.

2/that the *St. Mary* was running up and down the lower river two or three times a week all this time, while the Mackeys were cooling their heels in Bellevue OR 3/that there was another vessel by the same name, upon which the huge crowd of Mormons traveled.

But back to Sarah's Diary:

> *June 18th.* We are bussy preparing letters for home, we will leave them at Sioux City, it is the last chance we will have till we reach Fort Pierre.
>
> *June 21st.* Very winday, do not get along very fast. Jane, the babe's nurs is very sick today. Mrs. Chauteau has to take charge of it her self.
>
> This afternoon we got on a sanbar about four o'clock & did not get off till eight, which prevented us from reaching the Yancktons, a tribe of the Sioux Indians.
>
> *June 22nd.* Reached the Yancktons this morning about six o'clock, they came down from their loges, the chiefs & men amounting to three or four hundred came on the boat, they treated them to biscuit & coffee, after which Colonel Vaughan held a councle with them, after which he distribeted the U. S. Stores, which he had for them, the women and children were siting on the bank outside.
>
> We have had a dull Sabbath without preaching. Elkanah consulted a friend and fellow passenger about the propriety of speaking to the officers about preaching. He had been talking to the Capton (that is Dr. Steavans,)[93] he gave the Dr. to understand that it would

---

[93] The sense of this seems to be that "Dr. Steavens," the fellow passenger with whom Elkanah consulted spoke to the Captain (Joseph LaBarge), and, after speaking with the Captain, told Elkanah the Captain would not agree to let him preach.

That this was indeed about church loyalties may be inferred by Father De Smet's account of Charles Chouteau setting aside a

not be agreeable, So as all the officers & Mr. Chouteau and family were Roman Catholics, he thought it best to say nothing further on the subject unless it was mentioned to him.

June 23rd. Got out of ice to day, can not get any till we reach Fort Pierre, which will be four or five days, got on a sandbar about noon & did not get in the chanell of the river agan for several hours, they went ashore as soon as they could, then the Capton, with four or five other men, went out in a skiff to sound the water so that [they] could find the chanell, we all went ashore & amused ourselves in looking at the little pebbles which had washed ashore, we did not find many curiosities thoug[h], that were worth keeping. Some, or all the gentle men which were with us clambered up the bank, we sat under the shade of a tree till they came back, in about an hour after that they stoped again for wood, when we stoped they saw two or three men on the other side of the river before we got ready to start They were Indians, they were across on the Minosota side where we were stoped, one of them came abord the boat; he said he swam across. The other two came over in their canoe. They were very hungry, they gave him a pretty large poke of different kinds of food & a good deal of tobacca, with several other things, he was so glad. It is now almost dark, we are stoped for the night.

June 24th. Met the boat *Wm. Baird* [94] early this morning. Gen. Harney and a number of U.S. Officers were on board going down to Sioux City to hold a court marshall over an offercer charged with neglect of duty. He and some of his officers came on board our boat. Dr.

---

chapel for him on *Spread Eagle* in 1862, in order that he could celebrate daily mass as they ascended the river. -- *The Jesuits of the Middle United States*, Vol 2 Gilbert J Garraghan, p 364.

I am unable to identify "Dr. Steavens".

[94]A stern-wheel boat operating on the Missouri from 1855 to 1858. It sank at Waverly, Mo., in 1858. – *Coll. of KSHS,* Vol 9.

Ruther[95] , one of our passengers who was going up to Fort Pierre to see his daughter, the wife of one of the offercers of the army, very unexpectedly learned that his daughter & son- in-law were on board the *Wm. Baird*. He was waked out of a sound sleep to greet her, and in the expressive language of Mrs. Chouteau went into a series of conniptions when she spoke about the grandchild, Dr. Ruther, of cours, had himself & baggage transferred to the *Wm. Beard* and we lost a very pleasant companionable passenger, He is a brother of the Rev. Mr. Ruther, [96] a Presbyterian minister, who preaches at Chestnut Level.

June 25th. Stoped to take in wood; we all went ashore and had a delightful ramble. Reached Fort Lookout [97] about four o'clock where we found the St[eam]. boat *A. C. Godin* [98] just about to return to St. Louis, sent a short letter by her to Mother. We left that evening.

June 26th. Proceeding on fast towards Fort Pierre, very hot day & out of ice, the water was so warm it was hardly fit to drink. Wrote letter to Sammy, one to Amelia

---

95 Sarah writes it and Wilmer Mackey Sanney transcribes it as Ruther. The name is actually Rutter.

96 Lindley Charles Rutter was pastor in the 1850s at Chestnut Level Presbyterian Church in what is now Quarryville, Lancaster Co., PA. He was one of the founders of Chestnut Level Academy during that period.

97 During the period 1838 to 1858 "Fort Lookout" referred to a location on the west bank of the Missouri River several miles north of the mouth of White River. . ." In the vicinity of Fort Lookout, on the east side of the Missouri River, a trading post for the Yanktons was located." -Sioux Nation et al . . .vs USA, August 25, 1977, p.477.

98 *A.C. Goddin* Jack Ivers, master. A popular boat in her day. She sunk at Bonhomme Island, above St. Charles, April 20, 1857. - *Coll. of KSHS,* Vol 9

Emma and Dora, Elkanah wrote one to Wm. Armstrong.[99]

June 27th. Reached Fort Pierre about three o'clock. This is the highest point at which there is a P.O. Recived letters from home. We hoped this but scarcely dared to expect it. As we have a good deal of fraight to put off we may not get off till tomorrow. We walked out in the evening to see the Indians.

June 28th. We remained at Fort Pierre till evening about five o'clock. An Indian medicine man came into the ladies' Cabben & sat looking a long time at the ladies, appearing to be very much pleased, we asked him through an interpreter why he looked at us so much. He replied when we see a beautiful object a great distance away on the prairie we like to come near to it and look at it a great while. We stoped about sundown to take in wood & ice. Some of us went ashore to take a walk & speak to the Indians, a large number having assembled on the banks of the river. Before we returned to the boat a great wind storm arose.

The cable which fassend the boat to the shore broke loose, the boat came very near drifting down the river and leaving us among the Indians. Some of the Indians, however & the men that were on shore seased the roape. After a considerable effort the boat was again secured and we were glad to get on board as quick a possible.

June 29th. Another dull Sabbath, without any preaching.

In conversing with Mrs. Culbertson, through Mr. Culbertson, she told us she was nobody here among so many white ladies, but when she got among her own people she would be Mrs. Mackey's friend. We were

---

[99] An ambitious genealogist needs to identify these family members. Elsewhere Sammy is identified as "brother" and Emma as "sister".

obliged to tie up three or four hours today for the first time on account of the high wind.

June 30th. Nothing unusual occurred today, only we were wind-bound a few hours again. We went out and had a walk, got some very nice ripe black currants resembling those in the east, only something larger.

July 1st. Wrote a letter to sister Emma. Great change, yesterday a very cool & it is very hot today, the thermometer stands at ninety-six. -- Colonel Vaughan gave Elkanah a pair of Mockasins, and was going to give a pair but they were too large, he said he would give me a pair when we reached Fort Clark.

Elkanah's Journal entry for that day, later published in *The Home and Foreign Record* article quoted, indicates he was having some trouble with his eyes:

Above Fort Prairie, July 1st, 1856

I will commence writing to you now, so that without using my eyes too much at a time I may be able to say what I wish to before leaving the boat. Oh! that my eyes were sound, that I might address myself with vigour and industry to writing and study! But cease, repining thought! It is doubtless all for the best. A merciful Father has promised that all things shall work together for good to those that love him, and we should be content to be nothing and do nothing or anything that may be in accordance with his holy will.

Even our own narrow and short-sighted experience often shows us that in cases in which we would *at the time* have desired the dealings of Providence to be otherwise, afterwards we have seen that it was best for us that our desire were thwarted. Several times since we left home we have had occasion for thankfulness in this respect. I will only mention one instance.

We left Bellevue on the morning of the 17th of June, having been detained there four weeks and two days. We were kept in a state of suspense and felt some anxiety to get on for two or three weeks before the boat arrived. When we got up to Fort Pierre, however, on last Thursday, we found that the monthly mail had arrived just the day before and brought us a package of letters from our friends at home. We had heard nothing after leaving St. Louis, and if we had reached Fort Pierre two days sooner we would not have heard from there. Then we thanked God from our hearts that we had been detained.

Sarah's Diary continued:

July 2nd. Came to two bands of the Sioux today. The Yancktonies, a very large band when the boat stoped they were all seated in rows on the bank and commenced & sang as hard as they could yell to show that they were pleased, some of the Chiefs came in & had a councle with the agent who distributes the Government goods to them. When they found their goods had been left at Fort Pierre they were very angery. But after a long talk & giving a little provision, they were better satisfyed.

In the afternoon we came to another small band called the Two Solger [Soldier] band. They looked very poor, after the counsel was over two of the chiefs gave their Buffalo robes away one to Colonel Vaughn their father as they call him, & the other to Mr. Culbertson. This seemed like a noble act to me.

July 3rd. We got along very nicely to day, but nothing of special note occurred.

July 4th. This did not seem much like the fourth. In the morning they fired three cannons, through the day there was a good deal of drinking done, they talked of haveing some speaking in the evening, but it all fel through.

Alexander Culbertson by John Mix Stanley, about 1854

Elkanah's Journal entry written above Fort Pierre included his own observations about the *St. Mary*:

> Our boat [*St. Mary*] is much larger and pleasanter than we supposed it would be. We like it much better than the [Edinburgh]. The officers are very gentlemanly and unusually free from profanity for men in their station. And another thing that adds greatly to our enjoyment is, that Mr. Chouteau has his family along, i.e. Mr. Charles Chouteau, a son of Pierre Chouteau, Jr.
>
> Colonel Vaughan, the United States Agent for the Sioux and other tribes along the river, is on board. We

have stopped and held conferences with several bands of Sioux. They seem to be in a very destitute and almost

Alfred Jefferson Vaughan, Blackfoot Agent 1857, Shown here in uniform as Confederate Brigadier General in the Civil War.

starving condition, and the *year's supply* of provisions sent to them by the United States will scarcely be enough to last them one week. They do not seem disposed to work, and even if they were, their country is so barren that it would scarcely produce anything.

This part of the country is very different from what I supposed. Soon after we came above Sioux city, until a hundred miles above Fort Pierre, the country on both sides of the river is almost as barren as the sands of a great desert. We have frequent opportunity for observing it, particularly by roaming over the prairie every day when the boat stops to take in wood. And those who have been over the country, of whom there are several on the boat, say that back from the river, all through the country, it is as bad or worse. The country through which we are passing now is rather less barren and rugged than it was lower down. There is a very extensive region here that I have no idea will ever be fit for settlement or cultivation.

The impression I got from Mr. Culbertson at St. Louis was, that if the boat got up three hundred miles above Fort Union to Milk River, he would then proceed on with us by land. I think you [apparently the journal was addressed to Walter Lowrie at these "personal" points] had the same impression. He intends, however, to return by the boat to Fort Union, and will be detained there some weeks to attend to his business before he proceeds to Fort Benton.

Mrs. Culbertson and Fanny, their little daughter, joined us at Fort Pierre. We are very much pleased with them. Fanny is a bright, active, little girl of five years old. Mrs. Culbertson seems to be a woman of character and strong common sense. She says: "When I am on the boat here among all these white ladies I'm nobody; but when we get up to the Blackfeet country, then I'll be Mrs. Mackey's friend, and Mrs. Mackey will be a *siksika-ka,*" i. e. a Blackfeet lady.

We will have an express up to Fort Benton in October, and may have another in February. We hope to hear from you before a reinforcement comes on. Write us whether we shall select a site and commence preparations for building before a reinforcement arrives. We ought to commence to prepare early in spring, as it will be quite late in the season before a reinforcement can get up.

They reached Fort Clark on the 5th of July. This fort was described a few years earlier by Alexander's nephew, Thaddeus A. Culbertson:

> About six o'clock this morning we came in sight of Fort Clark; it is a small fort, about one-hundred feet in length on each side, and stands on the left bank [100] of the Missouri just below the Ree village. As we came around the bend a number of patches of ground under cultivation appeared along the river, and a very pleasing view was presented by the prairie curving inward for several miles, and the inner bank having the fort and village on it. [101]

This was also near the point where Jedidiah Smith offered the first Christian prayer of record on the upper Missouri on 2 June 1823. This was during a burial service for one of William Ashley's company, John Gardner, killed in a battle with the Arickarees. Hugh Glass, one of the leaders, wrote the young man's parents.

> My painfull duty it is to tell you of the deth of yr son who befell at the hands of the indians 2d June in the early morning. . . Mr. Smith a young man of our company made a powerful prayr wh moved us all greatly and I am persuaded John died in peace. [102]

---

100 In the parlance of river travel "left" and "right" banks are labelled in reference to downstream travel or as though one were facing downstream.

101 "Journal of an Expedition to the Mauvaises Terres and the Upper Missouri in 1850," by Thaddeus A. Culbertson, edited by John Francis McDermott. Smithsonian Institution, *Bureau of American Ethnology, Bulletin 147* (pp 95-6) U.S. Govt. Print Off. 1952

102 Hugh Glass to father of John S. Gardner, [June 1823, Box 3536A. Folder H75.14, State Archives, SDSHS. Timothy G. Anderson says it was particularly precious to South Dakota State Historian Doane Robinson, who published Glass's letter as part of the historical society's collection, (in 1901) and that John G. Neihardt also quoted

Elkanah's Journal continues:

> *July 5th.* – To-day Mr. Dawson, who has the superintendence at Fort Benton, got on the boat at Fort Clark. He is a Scotchman. Our first impressions of him were very favourable, and he is said to be a very fine man. He seems to be much pleased at our going up. When he found that we were going, he concluded at once to take with him his little son, a boy of about five years old. His mother was an Arickaree, and died when he was a baby, and he has been brought up at Fort Clark. We will find a number of half breeds in and about the Fort whose fathers will, no doubt, want them educated. When we start a boarding-school a question will arise as to the number of these that should be admitted.

Curiously a biography of Joseph La Barge indicates quite the contrary to the Mackeys "first impression" of Andrew Dawson, based on an incident supposed to have occurred at that place and time:

> In spite of saving this steamboat in which the American Fur Company owned half interest and other services he performed, LaBarge ended his employment with the company in the same year [1856]. This parting of the ways stemmed from an incident involving the chief clerk of the *St. Mary,* one of the sons of the partners in the fur company. The clerk's wife went along on a trip under the protection of LaBarge. At Fort Clark, the "bourgeois," or head of the post came aboard to travel to Fort Union.

---

from it in *The Splendid Wayfaring.* This from: "Memorializing a Mountain Man: John G. Neihardt, Doane Robinson, and Jedediah Smith" by Timothy G. Anderson, University of Nebraska 3-1-2009, online.

To make room for the man, two junior clerks were put out of their stateroom to sleep on cots elsewhere. The "bourgeois" resented this, and, holding an important post in the fur company hierarchy, said he would commandeer the lodging of the chief clerk, with pointed reference to the young man's wife. That night LaBarge allowed the bully to get as far as the cabin door, then collared him and literally kicked him to the other end of the boat. He ordered the crew to put the man off to spend the remainder of the night in the willows along the shore.

When the *St. Mary* returned to St. Louis, the young wife at once called on Mrs. LaBarge to thank her for the captain's gallant protection. In the meantime, the clerk proved himself an ungrateful coward by omitting all reference to LaBarge's chivalry and submitted to his father an official report that the captain was guilty of severe conduct to the company's employees. The report led to LaBarge's dismissal from the company.

He accepted the disgrace silently and, in three years, when the father learned the truth, he called on the captain to apologize and attempted to repair the damage caused by his son's actions. LaBarge declined the offers of the father and did not rejoin the fur company. [103]

Andrew Dawson seems to have been the "bourgeois" at Fort Clark at that time, going upriver to take that post at Fort Benton. The "chief clerk" could be Charles Chouteau, whose father was a partner in the American Fur Company. But Elkanah Mackey could hardly have escaped hearing about such events, and would not have spoken favorably of Dawson if he had heard about them. It seems likely that the incident, if it

103 "Joseph LaBarge Steamboat Captain" , T. S. Bowdern, S.J. *The Missouri Historical Review* published by the State Historical Society of Missouri, Columbia, Missouri, Vol 62, Summer 1968, pp. 449-469

occurred, was in a different year, or at least a different voyage of the St. Mary, probably with different characters. It is elsewhere attested, however, that Dawson had a reputation as a heavy drinker.

Andrew Dawson, American Fur Company employee. Factor or "Bourgeois" at Fort Benton in 1856

Andrew Dawson's move from Fort Pierre to Fort Benton was due to a big change of which Elkanah may not have been aware Fort Pierre had been sold to the War Department, and thus began the military "pacification" of the upper Missouri.

The American Fur Company, in 1855, sold Fort Pierre to the United States government. This prompted the beginning of the military conquest of the upper Missouri country and Joseph LaBarge, with a new boat named the *St. Mary*, moved the fur company out to a new post and returned to bring the army to the newly acquired fort.[104]

Sarah Mackey's Diary at this point sounds as though she felt very comfortable in her new surroundings:

> *July 5th.* We reached Fort Clark about nine o'clock today & did not lieve till after diner. Mr. Bennet & Mr. Mackey took us out to see the Fort & the Indian village, we had a great time, the Indians all followed us & looked at every road we turned, they were delighted & astonished to see so many white ladies. We found their lodges cleaner than we expected too, yet they seemed destitute of comfort. They admired my curls very much.

> *July 6th.* This did not seem like the Sabbath day, there was so much excitement & noise all day, we came to another band of Indians called the Gros. Ventres. I did not see much of them as I kept my room closely all day. Just when we were about to lieve the smoke pipe broke and we floated about a half mile down the river. We were obliged to stay the remander of the day, got ready to start in the morning.

---

[104]" Joseph LaBarge Steamboat Captain ".
Note: The new American Fur post was about 20 miles up the Missouri from Fort Pierre, at Chantier Creek.

CHAPTER THREE -- Birds of Passage

At Fort Pierre, a number of other passengers came aboard the *St. Mary*. Among them were topographers and a naturalist who was to become famous for launching a major movement in paleontology:

> On June 28, the geologist and medical doctor Ferdinand V. Hayden, and meteorologist J. Hudson Snowden boarded the AFC's steamboat *St. Mary* to explore upriver. Hayden, a small, energetic young man, had been scouring this region for fossils since 1853. When he joined [Lt. Gouverneur] Warren's 1856 expedition, he was famous in scientific circles for his Upper Missouri discoveries.[105]

The previous year, from his new base at Fort Pierre, Gen. William S. Harney had delivered a very severe blow in the form of a surprise attack against the Sioux at Ash Hollow or Blue Water Creek. It was intended to be uncompromisingly harsh, in keeping with the theory that the Indians would only submit after decisive defeat - and it was harsh indeed.

Lieutenant Gouverneur [the latter is his name not his title] K. Warren who looked down upon the aftermath from a hilltop, wrote in his journal that the sight was heartrending. He saw:

> " . . .wounded women & children crying & moaning, horribly mangled by the bullets" meant for the warriors

---

105 *Terrible Justice: Sioux Chiefs and U.S. Soldiers on the Upper Missouri, 1854–1868* by Doreen Chaky. University of Oklahoma Press, 2014 .

whose cover they sought to share. He rescued and tended as best he could two wounded women, a baby, two young girls, and two boys while the army surgeon and his assistants gave other rescued women and children "all the attention that skill and humanity could bestow." [106]

Gouverneur K. Warren, shown here in uniform as Union General in the Civil War, "The Hero of Little Roundtop"

Due largely to the complete surprise of the early morning attack, Harney only had four men killed, seven wounded, and one missing.

---

[106] *Terrible Justice. . .*

Fort Pierre, from am 1854 watercolor by Frederick Behman

The Sioux thus were so far beaten down that they submitted when Harney introduced Warren as the leader of this 1856 topographical expedition, warning them not to impede his party as it traveled through their country.

> Five feet six and weighing little more than 125 pounds, the twenty-six year old lieutenant probably did not impress the Indians as he stood next to the towering Harney, but the dark-haired officer stood erect and was said to be "poised and striking in appearance." He had graduated second in his West Point class and was already a rising star in the topographical corps.[107]
>
> . . . After helping to lay out Fort Lookout, Warren and topographer Hutton returned to Fort Pierre. [108]

---

107 *Terrible Justice . . .*

108 *Terrible Justice. . .*

There Hayden and Snowden joined them, and the expedition continued on up the river, eventually disembarking 60-80 miles above Fort Union.

Ferdinand Vandeveer Hayden, discoverer of the first American dinosaur remains to be described.

The paleontological report for which Hayden was to become most famous was based on his fossil collections made the previous year, in 1855. Apparently working then for himself and Indian agent Alfred Vaughan, he made his most striking discovery in the "Bad Lands of the Judith River, Nebraska Territory".[109]

[109] Title: *Various notices of fossil remains of fish, reptiles, and mammals, etc. discovered by Dr. F.V. Hayden in the Bad Lands of the Judith River, Nebraska Territory,* published in the *Proc. Acad. Nat. Sci.*, Phila., 1856, viii, and some of them also in *Amer. Jour. Sci.* xxi and xxii.

J. V. Hayden

The Judith River in "Nebraska Territory" is the Judith River in present Montana – as evidenced by the reference in the official version of the 1855 Stevens Treaty which was signed "near the mouth of the Judith River, in the territory of Nebraska". (The Mackeys would visit this spot for another Indian gathering in a few months.)

The Mackeys traveled together with Warren and Hayden from Fort Pierre to Fort Union, and perhaps on the jaunt beyond. Warren was to become the "Hero of Little Roundtop" in the Civil War [110], and Hayden's discoveries were to herald a major American obsession:

> In the year 2006 paleontologists will celebrate the 150th anniversary of the first description of a dinosaur fossil from North America. In March 1856 Joseph Leidy of Philadelphia wrote a brief paper describing and naming four kinds of 75-million-year-old[111] reptilean teeth that had been discovered the previous year in the Cretaceous beds of the Judith River region of Montana . . .
>
> . . .they included incomplete teeth of Deinodon [horridus] and Trachodon . . .[112]

---

[110] Gouverneur K. Warren of the Corps of Topographical Engineers, also drew the first comprehensive map of the American West, a major step in American cartography. It was published in 1858.

[111] The age suggested here is a more recent "discovery".

[112] "American Dinosaurs: Who and What Was First," by Keith Stewart Thomson copyright 2006. Sigma Xi, The Scientific Research Society. Online at: www.americanscientist.org.

Lieutenant Warren later described the route his 1856 expedition was to take:

> . . .[I was accompanied by] Mr. N. H. Hutton and Mr. J. H. Snowden, assistant topographers, Dr. and F.V. Hayden [one and the same person], geologist and naturalist, and was provided with an astronomical transit, a sextant, chronometers, barometers, odometers, and compasses. We started on a steamboat [*Genoa*][113] from St. Louis, April 16, to join General Harney at Fort Pierre, and on our way made a map of the Missouri from the mouth of the Big Nemeha. At Fort Pierre I received orders from General Harney to proceed on board the American Fur Company's boat *St. Mary*, and examine the Missouri river as far as she should go, . . .

As interesting as he may have found these frontiersmen, Elkanah's Journal indicates he was paying more attention to the lifestyle of the Indians he was meeting:

---

113 "Although the journey to Fort Pierre began on the steamer *Genoa*, it ended as a long hike. Warren enjoyed riverboat travel but grew impatient as the *Genoa* struggled against wind and current. Finally, when the vessel ran aground on a sandbar in the shallows near the mouth of Running Water, he, the Fort Pierre sutler, and three others set out overland for the post. They walked 160 miles, subsisting mainly on birds brought down with shotguns. Although the journey was hard, Warren welcomed the chance to examine the terrain away from the river. On 21 May 1856, the lieutenant reported to Colonel Harney at Fort Pierre. He and his companions had beaten the *Genoa* by three days." *Vanguard of Expansion: Army Engineers in the Trans-Mississippi West, 1819-1879* by Frank N. Schubert, chapter VII.

July 7th. – The Arickarees and Mandans that we passed on Saturday, and the Gros Ventres that we saw yesterday, are permanently located, and raise a great deal more corn and beans than they need for their own consumption. They have thus a permanent means of subsistence, and are certainly in a better condition to be civilized than the nomadic tribes. The Arickarees number eight hundred and have their villages at Fort Clark. The Mandans number two hundred and fifty, and are located about three miles above. Could not a missionary be provided for these two tribes?

The Gros Ventres are at Fort Berthold, and number seven hundred and fifty. I have had a conversation with one of their principle chiefs. He says he would be very glad to have white men and women to come and live among them and teach them to read God's book, and write, and be like white men. He is a noble, honest looking man. Could not a missionary be got to go there? I told him I could not promise to send him one, but that I would try. We passed several bands of the Sioux last week, farther down the river. They, too, look haggard and are in a wretched and almost starving condition.

The more I reflect upon it, the more I am convinced that the proper course in Christianizing the Indian is to send missions to those remote from the *corrupting influence of civilization*.

Sarah's Diary for the same days indicates she was fascinated by the animal life:

July 7th. Saw the first Buffalo today. It was a fine big fellow which we soon lost sight of as it ran over the hill. Soon afer, we saw a large herd on an Island. They were frightened by the steam boat & plunged into the water & swam away to the opisit side, there was a great many shots fired at them but they escaped unhurt. In the evening the men shot & brought in two deer.

> *July 8th.* Saw any quanity of Buffalo today & had quite an exciting time. There was two on the edge of the river & confined there by a high bank. The poor things were badly frightened & they had good reason to be, for there was more than fifty guns ready to fire on them. One of them was killed and the other escaped with life but not without being wounded, it was able to run when it got across the river to the great joy of many who were looking on. There was a simelar scene in the afternoon.
>
> In the afternoon when the boat was stoped to take in wood, our hunter, Mr. Cadotte went out a hunting, he returned to the boat in about two hours having slaughtered four Buffalo and a Deer.
>
> *July 9th.* Nothing unusual occured to day.

Finally they arrived at Fort Union, their penultimate destination. And Sarah was quite ready to get off the steamer:

> *July 10th.* Got to the mouth of the Yellow Stone about four o'clock. Crossed over to the Fort, unloaded the freight for that place. Mr. Culbertson sent for his carriage and took us all out a riding, which was a great treat after being so long confined in the boat.

But the very next day, for reasons they did not give, the Mackeys went along as St. Mary headed on up the Missouri. The main reason for extending the boat's trip was transporting supplies to the Indian annuity distribution and to Fort Benton. Either the Mackeys went along just to see more of the country, or possibly Mr. Culbertson hoped the river would prove high enough that he could get them well on their way to Fort Benton by this mode of transportation. Elkanah mentioned earlier that Culbertson had spoken of going three hundred miles further.

Sarah wrote:

July 11th. Left Fort Union this morning to go higher up the river, made a fine day's run.

Elkanah also made some journal entries:

July 11th. – Yesterday afternoon, at four o'clock, we passed the mouth of the Yellow Stone, and soon after reached Fort Union, which is two miles above. We have left the freight which was intended for that point, and are now on our way up the river with the goods intended for Fort Benton. They intend to go as high as they can, but do not know how high. Our trip thus far has been on the whole a very pleasant one, much pleasanter than we had anticipated.

Our heartfelt gratitude is due to the kind Providence that has smoothed our way thus far, and we will trust him for the future. I will finish this before we leave the boat.

Major Hatch, the United States Agent to the Blackfeet joined us at Fort Union and is now on board.

July 12th. – We went about ninety miles above Fort Union; have unloaded all the goods, and now, four o'clock are on our way back to Fort Union. Mr. Culbertson thinks now he will not be detained there more than two weeks. The charge for our passage on the boat is $120. I gave Captain La Barge a draft for that amount. Sarah as well, and joins me in love to all our friends in New York. We hope to hear from you this fall, but the February express, they say, is very doubtful.[114]

---

[114] ibid.

NOTE: Much of the contents were unknown to me until I found Wilmer Mackey Sanner's book. The second half of Elkanah's records, including his "Private Letter" and "Report" are at the Presbyterian Historical Society, Philadelphia.

This "there and back again" jaunt was also given brief coverage in Sarah's Diary:

> *July 12th.* Got about one hundred miles above Fort Union where we unloaded all the freight in the edge of the woods where we left the hands there who were to take the freight in the Mackinaws. On leaving them fired three cannons & they gave three cheers, poor fellows, they have hard work before them. We are now on our way to Fort Union, will probily reach there this everning or early in the morning.
>
> *Monday, July 14th.* Reached Fort Union yesterday [13th] about eight o'clock. The carriage came down from the Fort to take us up. I was not quite ready to go, so they made up a lode without us & came back for us.

Sarah then records what sounds like her most difficult parting thus far:

> Mrs. Chouteau, [115] all her family & Mrs. McDonald, stayed with us at the Fort till the boat was almost ready to start.
>
> We became very much attached to them all. Mrs. Chauteau was very kind, she presented us with her Medicine Chest, thinking we might need it in travaling across the cuntry. This was a great favour as we had our medicines all most all packed where we could not get them. Old Jany, little Ms.[?] Nanny's [116] nurse, was very attentive to me. She always made me a cup of tea when I did not feel very well. They were all as kind as they could be.
>
> Their company added much to the pleasure of our trip. But Ah! the parting. I cannot dwell on that -- it brings too vividly before my mind the separation from

---

[115] Julia Augusta Gratiot married Charles Chouteau in 1845.

[116] Charles and Julia's daughter, Nannie, was born on January 4, 1856.

> our beloved relatives. But, now came the last long farewell.
>
> We stood on the river's brink, the boat moved off. This was a trying hour, this seemed like the last link of Civelization & we were taking our last look on the face of a white lady for at least one year. We wached her through tears as she moved off. But we were strengthened & sustained by that same Father who has always taken care of us & by the precious promis of the Savior, "Lo, I am with you alway."
>
> We returned to our room hoping to enjoy the Sabbath evening in quietness. But a number of men in the Fort were drunk, profanity, noise & disorder were the concequence.
>
> We occupy the upper rooms in the east wing of the large house on the north side of the Fort.

Sarah's transparence is disarming. She is so obviously aware that hers was the last white female face in the company. Apart from her husband, *Natoyist Siksina'* Culbertson was now to be her closest companion. Indeed the next day they spent together:

> [*14th*] Today we took a ride with Mrs. Culbertson, down to Fort Wm. We had delightful ride & as we were going, the Assinaboins were just coming over the hill with all their things. They were coming near the Fort to encamp to receive their Government goods.
>
> It was the prettiest scene I had witnessed. They had their dogs hitched to their lodge poles in the form or in the place of a wagon, on these they fasten their goods & hall them with their dogs, poor things, some of them were so tired they were laying down. They got over it, however, very soon. Such a yowling or howling of dogs I never herd, nor such a quanity a never saw before, they looked as though they would number one thousand, they had very few horses. As we returned they had their

lodges up, we drove around to see them. I was presented with two fur Mockasins at the Fort, but they are too large for me. Mr. Mackey thinks it is very fortunate for him that I have such a little foot, as he falls heir to all my Mockasins.

In his next letter to Walter Lowrie, Elkanah describes the Culbertsons, dwelling particularly on Mrs. Culbertson. Alexander's wife was and is sometimes commonly referred to as "Natawista," a somewhat garbled

Captain Joseph La Barge, Master of *St. Mary*, One of the most respected Missouri river pilots

version of *Natuyizixina* or *Natoyist Siksina'*, which means "Sacred Snake" Woman. [117] She was indeed a Blackfoot "princess," called that by John James Audubon,[118] and well-attested as related to many of the Blood (Kainah) leaders, and to leaders of the other Blackfoot tribes.

The Chouteaus having departed, the weather and various activities among the Indians and agents occupied Sarah's observations at Fort Union:

> *Tuesday, July 15th.* Last night we had a heavy thunder gust. Today we went out to the Indian Council. Heard Col. Vaughan's palaver with the Chiefs of the Assinaboins.
>
> *Wednesday, July 16th.* A severe thunder gust last night & it has been raining very heavy all day and still continues to rain. The roof leaks & lets the water in on one side of our room which makes it look a little dismal but we are very glad we are not on the Prairie.
>
> We have a fire place in our roome in which we have a very cheerful fire which helps to take away the dampness & dullness.
>
> *Thursday, July 17th.* It cleared off last night. The rain was greater than it is usually here at one time. This afternoon we went a fishing. I caught a clever sized catfish and a sturgeon near two feet long. The latter I sent to the Smithsonian Institute through Dr. Hayden. [119]

---

[117] Jack Holterman, LTR, to author, 15 January 1982. See also *King of the High Missouri*, , CH X, "Queen of the High Missouri", p. 57.
[118] Holterman, *King of the High Missouri,* CH X, p. 57. Natawista met Audubon when he went up the Missouri to Fort Union on the Omega in 1843. There he painted portraits of each of them. Alexander and Natawista later visited Audubon at his estate on the Hudson river in New York. See also Holterman, pp. 61, 69.
[119] Wilmer Mackey Sanner researched these specimens, and gives details about Dr. Hayden's Smithsonian contributions of that year.

Friday July 18th. Dr. Hayden called in our room this morning, had a long talk on Indian languages. Mr. Bennet came in to get a needle to fasten a buton on his shirt, as he had been trying it for a long time without success with one to large for the eye.

We all went a fishing this afternoon again. I had no luck, Mr. Mackey caught a fine catfish.

Saturday, July 19th. The Assinaboins invited us to a dog feast today. Mr. Mackey & I declined going, for several reasons.

This evening they came in the Fort and gave us a very interesting dance, it was amusing to see them all fixed off in their odd stile, then they had such strange motions. And yet it made me feel sad to see so many noble looking men all so ignorant and destitute of the comforts of life.

By the way, I forgot to mention the Buffalo dance of Thursday [*17th*]. It looked very savvage to see them come into the yard with Buffalo heads on their heads. Some of them were dressed off grand in there stile & others were almost entirely naked. They all had muskets loaded with powder and every round of dancing they shot them, generally among themselves, but sometimes at a dog which would make it run & yell. They always expect some presents from some of the whites who are present on such an occasion. They received a good deal on that occasion.

Monday, July 21st. Yesterday Mr. Mackey preached in the Fort to an audience of thirty persons who were very attentive hearers.

The next day, Elkanah wrote another letter to Mr. Lowrie:

Walter Lowrie, Esq. Fort Union
July 22nd 1856

Mrs. Culbertson, "Natawista" and child, from a portrait by John James Audubon and Isaac Sprague

My Dear Sir, We have been here now nine days & expect to leave for Fort Benton on the 25th. The Boat belonging to the opposition Fur Co. will be up to Fort Williams to-day.[120] Fort W. is two miles below Fort Union by land but by water not less than 8 or so. I embrace the opportunity furnished by this boat to drop you a few lines to inform you of our movements. Our circumstances here are quite comfortable. Mr.

---

[120] Holterman in his MSS chapter "Locust Grove" refers to the Culbertsons traveling on the *Robert Campbell* with Colonel Vaughan and other friends from St. Joseph. Elkanah states clearly they were traveling on the *St. Mary* from Bellevue.

> Culbertson & Mrs. Culbertson too do all they can to make it pleasant for us. I think she is a very remarkable woman, considering the opportunities she has had. She is very prudent & has the most deep-seated & persevering opposition to the use of liquor.

Elkanah goes on: "Last Sabbath I preached in the Fort to a congregation of 30 persons."

Fort Union, from a lithograph, by John Mix Stanley, in Isaac Stevens' 1853 Pacific Railroad Report

The Mackeys were not only getting to know the remarkable "Siksika-ka," Mrs. Culbertson, but at Fort Union, they were meeting more native Americans:

> The Assiniboines came in and encamped last week on the Prairie near the Fort for the purpose of receiving the annuities sent to them by government. On Wednesday [16th] Col. Vaughan the Gov. Agent went out to hold a council with the chiefs under cover of a skin lodge.
>
> Mr. & Mrs. Culbertson, Mrs. Mackey & I and some others accompanied him. They are very peaceably

disposed now. They have had some variance with the Blackfeet, but some 8 or 10 of the young men & some of the chiefs are staying here and intend to accompany us for the purposes of making a treaty of peace & friendship with the pipe of peace together.

With the exception of those few who remain here the Assiniboines have decamped & gone back to their hunting grounds. I had some conversation with some of their chiefs particularly with *Fool Bear*. He is a noble, fine looking man & exerts a great influence in his tribe. During the course of our conversations I asked him if he & his people believed in the existence of a God. He replied, Oh yes! Their Fathers had taught them to believe that and to pray to him. They were sure there must be a God, for what would be the use of praying to God if there were none.

I told him he was correct in his belief, that white men had God's Book, and asked him if they would be willing to have white men & women come & live among them & teach them how to read God's Book, and to worship him aright. He said they would be very glad to have them & would treat them kindly. Can not some branch of the Church of Christ send a mission to this tribe? They number between three & four thousand.

We have had occasion for thankfulness at being detained here as last week we had a very severe storm. We would no doubt have thought it much more so if we had met it on the prairie.

Truly and affectionately your & c. E. D. Mackey[121]

While at Fort Union, the Mackeys met more western characters, including two often numbered among "famous mountain men." These were James Kipp, American Fur "factor" at Fort Union, and Jim Bridger, who seems to have arrived at the fort just about the same

---

[121] ibid.

time as they. Kipp was in the midst of reinforcing the fort's outer walls, a log palisade, and was using a horse-powered sawmill to cut his lumber.[122]

James Kipp was born in 1788 near Montreal and entered the fur trade in the Red River region, from which he returned in 1813 to marry 19 year old Elizabeth Rocheleau. They settled in Montreal, where James Kipp worked five years as a carpenter, joiner and mason. By 1818 he was back in the fur trade, but now in the Upper Missouri River region.

In 1821, when the North West Company merged with the Hudson's Bay Company, and a number of men thus lost their positions, he was among those forming a new company, known as the Columbia Fur (Tilton and Company), led by Kenneth McKenzie and including Honoré Picotte.

Kipp became company agent in the country of the Mandans. His talents as a builder were frequently employed. In 1823 he seems to have built a post at the Mandan villages on the Missouri River where he and six other men were stationed. They weathered a dangerous period here in fall 1823 when large numbers of angry, displaced, Arickara Indians moved into the vicinity following the Leavenworth campaign.

In 1825/6, Kipp built another post at the mouth of White Earth River known as "Kipp's Post" or "Tilton's Post". When Columbia Fur Company merged with the American Fur Company in June of 1827, Kipp continued on with the new Upper Missouri Outfit, which tasked him in 1828 with constructing Fort Floyd, later known as Fort Union. He built Fort Clark at the Mandan villages in 1830-31. In the winter of 1831-1832, Kipp and crew went up to Blackfoot country, where they built Fort Piegan on the Marias River.

---

[122] Journal, Agent Edwin A.C. Hatch

In 1832, George Catlin, American painter of the aborigines of the American West, came to visit Fort Clark and lived with James Kipp, who hired him as clerk for a few months, and helped him in his research.

The following year, 1833, the German Prince, Alexander Philippe Maximilian of Wied-Neuwied, visited, describing a pow-wow in which:

> the pipe went round, and the conversation began with the Mandans, by the assistance of Mr. Kipp, clerk of the American Fur Company and the director of the trading post at Fort Clark.[123]

James Kipp left Fort Clark about 1835 and was dispatched to the upper Missouri where he was charged with the construction of Fort McKenzie to replace Fort Piegan which had been burned by the Blackfoots.

In 1838, he made his winter quarters in Platte County, on the Missouri, about ten miles north of Kansas City. In July 1844, he purchased farmland in Platte County, then bought more from Honoré Picotte near the town of Barry. "Captain Kipp" is said to have piloted a steam boat above Kansas City on the Missouri —around 1840.

In 1843, he was placed in charge of another company post, Fort Alexander, on the Yellowstone River, where the naturalist Audubon paid him a visit. And by 1845, James Kipp was in charge of American Fur's post at Fort Union.

Like many another American, Kipp spent time pursuing riches in California's gold rush of 1849, but soon returned to the fur trade on the Missouri. Thus by the summer of 1851 he was in charge of Fort Berthold back in the country of the Mandans. There he received a visit from

---

[123] *Travels in the Interior of North America, 1832-1834,* Volume 1 Maximilian von Wied. Arthur H. Clark Company, 1905. p345

a young Swiss naturalist and painter, Rudolph Friederich Kurz, whom he employed as a clerk for two months. According to Kurz, Kipp had both a white family in Missouri, and a Mandan woman and family.

A local newspaper announced the arrival of Captain Kipp at Liberty, the Missouri river landing place closest to his farm at Barry, on the 29th of July 1853.[124]

Kipp seems to have come up the river early the spring of 1856, possibly on the steamboat, *Genoa,* the laggardly speed of which had frustrated Lieutenant Warren and friends. [125]

Jim Bridger, for nearly two years prior to this, had been guiding a somewhat infamous Irish peer, Sir George Gore, who made himself variously unwelcome. Among the enemies he made were frontier military officers, the Indians, and the animals of Nebraska Territory, which he and his party were intent on dispatching in large numbers.

Indian Agent Vaughan was among many who were unhappy with the baronet. He wrote to his supervisor, the Indian Commissioner, and expressed his feelings:

> The English Gentleman [Gore] . . .will return in a month or so . . .having been in the Indian Country since the passport was issued by you 24th May 1854 . . .He has most palpably violated it. [With his men] forty-three in number, he built a Fort in the Crow country some 100 feet square and inhabited the same nine months, trading with the Crows . . . .He and his men also state that he

---

[124] *Liberty Tribune article* "Late from the Mountains"

[125] Various sources for these biographical notes on James Kipp include: "James Kipp: Upper Missouri River Fur Trader and Missouri Farmer". W. Raymond Wood. Published in *North Dakota History, Journal of the Northern Plains*, Vol. 77, Nos. 1 & 2. Pages 40, ND State Hist Soc., 2011; and , "James Kipp," Ray H. Mattison, in *The Mountain Men and the Fur trade of the Far West*, ed. Leroy R. Hafen, 3:167-72. Glendale, CA: Arthur H Clark, 1966; and an online site "The Kip/Kipp Family of New Amsterdam (New York)" on *Ancestry.com.*

> killed 105 bears and some 2000 buffalo; Elk and Deer, 1600 . . .purely for sport . . . .The Indians have been loud in their complaints . . .What can I do? . . . .Nothing, I assure you, beyond apprising you. [126]

Nor was Gore quite done with his western holiday. Nonetheless Jim Bridger was done with him. Perhaps as a more remunerative, or a more reputable alternative, Bridger accepted Lieutenant Warren's offer to guide his topographical party up the Yellowstone valley into Sioux country.

James Felix Bridger was born in Richmond, Virginia in 1804, son of an inn-keeper. His parents moved to St. Louis when he was eight, but four years later, both of them died. He became a blacksmith's apprentice, without formal education, but at 18 joined General Ashley's 1822 Upper Missouri Expedition, along with that other famous mountain man, Jedidiah Strong Smith. On this adventure, Bridger learned fur-trapping and trading, which accounted for his next twenty years.

His travels to and fro across the uncharted Rocky Mountain west lent him a familiarity with much of what are now eight western states and two Canadian provinces, with the Platte and Missouri rivers as his arterial

---

[126] A.J. Vaughan, Fort Union, July 1856, to Commissioner William Clark from *M. H. S. Contributions, Vol X*. Quoted in *Jim Bridger* , J. Cecil Alter

highways. He is credited with many discoveries, including the Great Salt Lake.

In 1830, Bridger and some fellow trappers bought out Jed Smith, who had succeeded Ashley. They named their company Rocky Mountain Fur, thus became "the opposition" to American Fur along the river, and Hudson Bay Company in the north. This competition furnished impetus to expand their territory into Blackfoot country, which resulted in further hostilities. By 1834, Bridger and partners gave up the enterprise and dissolved Rocky Mountain Fur, falling back on various frontier occupations.

In 1835 Bridger married Cora Insula, of the Flathead Indians, with whom he had three children.

Jim Bridger, noted mountain man

In 1843 Jim Bridger and Louis Vasquez built a post, later called Fort Bridger, on Black's Fork of the Green River, in what is now the southwest corner of Wyoming in order to cash in on the new Oregon Trail. They traded with travelers and with Indians. For several days in July 1846, they helped the ill-fated Donner party re-supply and repair their wagons before they began their fatal journey over an untried "short-cut" through the mountains. That year Bridger's first wife died in childbirth.

Bridger met Brigham Young and the first wave of Mormon pioneers in June 1847, with whom he shared his knowledge and reservations about settling in the Salt Lake area. At first the Mormon immigrants increased trade at the post, but soon Mormon settlements began to compete for Bridger's trade, both with travelers and Indians.

Charles Chouquette, who traveled with them overland and was to be Elkanah's guide at Fort Benton, recalled meeting Jim Bridger on the Upper Missouri in 1849, on Chouquette's first trip. They and 82 others fought a pitched battle with several times more Blackfoot warriors near present Great Falls.

> One of the most notable Indian battles in which Mr. Chouquette was engaged occurred in April, 1849, on the site of the city of Great Falls. He and Anton Bussette and Louis La Breche had fortunately joined the famous trapper, Jim Bridger, who had eighty men in his following. While in camp on the Missouri at the point mentioned they were fiercely attacked by 400 savages. . . and for a time the scale of battle hung about equally between the contending forces. At last the Indians were repulsed, leaving forty-seven of their companions dead on the field. This was during Mr. Chouquette's first trip

up the river, when he assisted in moving the stores of Fort William to Fort Benton.[127]

In 1850, Bridger married Shoshone Chief Washakie's daughter, Mary, "Little Fawn" with whom he had two more children. Some of his children were sent back east to be educated. That same year Bridger guided a Mormon expedition along what became the Overland Trail - just as Utah Territory was officially established, with Fort Bridger in its jurisdiction.

In the summer of 1853, Mormon leaders accused Bridger of illicit arms trade with the Indians. They revoked his right to trade and sent a posse to arrest him. Bridger fled and did not return to the mountains until 1855, at which juncture he sold his post to the Mormons.

The Mormons inaugurated a system of handcart companies in the spring of 1856, in order to enable poor European emigrants to make the trek more cheaply. Handcarts were two-wheeled carts that were pulled by emigrants instead of draft animals. Over several years, almost 3,000 Mormons, with 653 carts and 50 supply wagons, traveling in 10 different companies, made the trip over the trail to Salt Lake City. [128]

---

[127]pp 163-170 in Robert Vaughn's *Then and now; or, Thirty-six years in the Rockies. Personal reminiscences of some of the first pioneers of the state of Montana.* Indians and Indian wars. The past and present of the Rocky mountain country. 1864-1900. Attributed thusly, "The following sketch, from Charles Choquette, appeared in *The New York Sun* in the summer of 1899." --Apparently an interview long after the event.

[128] In October 1856, one of the first of these ran into early winter hardships. A rescuer, George E. Grant recorded, "You can imagine between five and six hundred men, women and children, worn down by drawing handcarts through snow and mud; fainting by the wayside; falling, chilled by the cold; children crying, their limbs stiffened by cold, their feet bleeding and some of them bare to snow and frost."

With his wide experience among various Indian tribes, including family ties to several, Bridger certainly would have seemed a valuable resource to Elkanah Mackey. We have no record of their conversations. Did they touch on spiritual things? Perhaps so, since Bridger's earliest western adventures were spent with Jedidiah Smith, whose letters reflect a heartfelt Christian faith.

It seems nearly certain the Mackeys met the Irish baronet, Sir George Gore at Fort Union, but we have no record of the meeting. We know from quite a few sources that Sir George was returning from a spectacular two year expedition fitted up chiefly for his sporting pleasure, and guided up to this point by Jim Bridger. Lt. James Bradley, an infantry officer described the Eighth Baronet of Manor Gore as, of medium height, but rather stout, bald with short side whiskers, a good walker but poor horseman."[129]

As Agent Vaughan's letter mentioned, Gore started out in May of 1854. His expedition went overland from St. Louis and up the North fork of the Platte river, where he wintered at Ft. Laramie. His was one of the biggest "hunting trips" in the history of the United States - not only in the size of the slaughter Vaughan mentions, but in the scale and duration of it.

Lieut. Bradley described the party as it went on from Fort Laramie in the spring of 1855, thus:

> Sir George left Laramie with forty-one men, four six-mule wagons, two three-yoke ox wagons and twenty-one French carts, painted red, each drawn by two horses. One wagon was loaded entirely with Sir

---

[129] "Sir George, the Buffalo Slayer," Hal Schindler, *Salt Lake Tribune* 02/16/1997 quoting Lt. James Bradley MSS, *M. H. S. Contributions,* Vol IX, 1923, p. 249. Note: the baronet's ancestor, Paul Gore, was a captain of horse under Elizabeth and James I, and he or his son was created baronet in 1622. The family motto was *Sola salus servire Deo.* -- To serve God is the only salvation.

> George's private arms, of which he had some seventy-five rifles with a large number, twelve or fifteen, shotguns, and two wagons with Sir George's fishing tackle. One of his attendants was a skilled fly maker and was constantly gathering new material for flies. Sir George was abundantly supplied with everything necessary to his convenience and comfort. He had a large linen tent, about ten by eighteen feet, hung throughout with striped lining, a brass bedstead that unscrewed and packed in a small space, a portable iron table and iron washstand, and three milk cows. He carried with him also a splendid telescope with about a six-inch lens, supported upon a tripod, an instrument of great power. . . . He also had a large number of pistols of every description including revolvers. [130]

The party left Fort Laramie and went up to the Yellowstone which they followed to the Tongue river, and built themselves the fort Vaughan mentions there. All along the way they fished and hunted, killing far more animals than they ate, and collecting trophies whenever they could. They wintered over 1855-56 at their own fort. One memorial to the Gore Expedition is said to be the town of Glendive, named for Glendive Creek, which the baronet named for a stream in Ireland of which it reminded him - possibly Glendale, originally.[131]

Then in the summer of 1856, Sir George's small army divided near the mouth of the Tongue River after building two flat-boats. [132] Sir George and a dozen or so men, set out down the Yellowstone in the boats laden with trophies, equipment and supplies. The majority of their party had gone overland on horses, taking the livestock. The destination of both groups was Fort Union, where

---

[130] Lieut. James Bradley MSS, pp.246-47

[131] There is a Glendale in the Scottish Isle of Skye, a vale in Duirinish parish, Inverness-shire.

[132] A flatboat is a smaller and flimsier version of the Mackinaw.

they reunited, apparently about the time *St. Mary* arrived.[133]

Meanwhile, either ahead of time, through messengers, or immediately upon arriving at Fort Union, Sir George contracted with the American Fur official(s) for an exchange. He wanted two Mackinaw boats from them on which to carry back his trophies and equipment and such of his crew as would fit aboard them. In return he pledged to give them his horses, livestock, wagons, carts, and such other supplies and equipment as he no longer wanted and/or could not carry in the boats. Some agreement had been reached which must have involved additional payment on one side or the other.

When Sir Gore got to Fort Union, the Mackinaws were either ready, or they were quickly built. It is tempting to speculate about this. [134] But someone -- either Kipp or Culbertson talked with Gore after the boats were presented and said something that made Gore angry. The negotiating official either modified the original agreement or clarified it from American Fur's standpoint in such a manner that Gore was convinced he was being bamboozled. This altercation literally produced a lot of heat in the end.

Different accounts leave us unsure if Sir George's ire was precipitated by and directed against James Kipp, or Alexander Culbertson. Kipp had already been at the post for a while that spring before the Culbertsons and Mackeys arrived aboard *St. Mary*. But Culbertson seems to have outranked him, and may have taken over the negotiations.

---

[133] Another interpretation of these events places them a month or two later, perhaps as Alexander Culbertson was returning downriver via Fort Union. This seems to be Jack Holterman's conclusion.

[134] – Was one of them the one built upriver at Fort Benton that spring? See the end of Chapter Four.

By all accounts, Jim Bridger got along with Sir George. He was a likable man to those who liked him. But also by all accounts the baronet was capable of being, "mercurial, wrathful, effervescent and reckless and heedless of consequences"[135] Gore's method for dealing with the situation at Fort Union was certainly all of that:

> . . . he would not stand the terms prescribed. He accordingly burned his wagons, and all the Indian goods and supplies not needed in front of the fort, guarding the flames from the plunder of whites and Indians." [136]

He even maintained a guard over the ashes of the colossal bonfire until they had cooled down, and then had his men throw all the iron hardware into the river so that the inhabitants of Fort Union would gain no benefit from them. Sir George sold or gave away his stock to hangers-on and Indians, and went on down the river to Fort Berthold in the two flatboats he had built. There he wintered over, causing a bit more discord, until he returned to St. Louis in the spring of 1857.

Apparently these circumstances did benefit one enterprise , however. Lieut. G. K. Warren recorded, apparently not chronologically:

> I made an examination of the Yellowstone River in August, 1856, and in carrying this out, I was fortunate in being able to purchase the means of land transportation from Sir George Gore, who was returning from an extensive hunting excursion .[137]

---

135 "Sir George Gore's Expedition (1854-56) from Conversations with Henry Bostwick, a Member of the Party" by F. Geo. Heldt , in *M. H. S. Contributions, Vol. 1.* Helena, Rocky Mountain Publishing Company, 1876. pp.144ff

136 ibid. "Sir George Gore's Expedition. . ."

137 *Jim Bridger*, J. Cecil Alter, University of Oklahoma Press, 2013. p.261.

Warren was also Jim Bridger's new employer. On July 25, 1856, Bridger led Warren and the scientists away from Fort Union. With them besides a seventeen man Second Infantry unit - were a hunter, a cook, laborers, mule drivers, and the scientists' assistants – a total of thirty-four armed and well-supplied men. . . . about to explore the Yellowstone to the mouth of Powder River.

For about two weeks before they left, the Mackeys were at Fort Union with all of these people, except for the short trip further up the river and back on the St. Mary.

Earlier boats had already brought loads of trade-goods and supplies to Fort Union. Wagons were sent on from Ft. Union in early June. We know this from the Fort Benton Journal, noting the arrival of these:

> *20 June* – Mr. Wray arrived with wagon at the mouth of the Maria River to[o] high to cross request boat. . .
> *21 June* – set a wagon with our boat to cross our goods at the Mouth of the Maria. Towards evening our wagons arrived with one wheel broken . . .[138]

Sarah's Diary also mentions the Warren expedition leaving Fort Union:

> *Friday, July 25th.* Nothing of importance occurred during the week except the arival of the *Clara* [139] at Fort Wm. & the departure at Col. Vaughan & party up the Yellow Stone. The *Clara* brought us a package of letters from our friends at home, which was a very unexpected treat. Thanks to the kind Providence for detaining us at Fort Union untill they came.

---

[138] *M. H. S. Contributions, Vol X,* "Fort Benton Journal"

[139] *Clara* (no. 1) J. Cheever, master. a side-wheel lower river passenger boat, of 248 tons, operated from 1851 to 1856. She was sunk by ice at St. Louis in 1856. — *Collections of Kansas State Historical Society*, Vol 9.

We sent letters down by the *Clara* which our friends will be very much surprised to recive as we did not expect to have that opportunity.

From a photograph once said to be of Mrs. Culbertson, but now thought to be of her daughter, Fanny.

CHAPTER FOUR - Overland to Fort Benton

Elkanah mentions an imminent departure delayed. They were about to set out overland from Fort Union to Fort Benton. Fort Union, in present North Dakota near the eastern border of Montana, was for all intents and purposes the furthest port of steamboat navigation on the Missouri until 1859, when the *Chippewa* became the first steamboat to land at Fort Benton. Steamboats had gone higher than Fort Union, however, as did *St. Mary* on this occasion. The rule was to go as far up as possible on the spring flood, when the river was swollen by the melting of mountain snow, and then arrange overland transportation for passengers and freight intended for higher "ports".

That year, the Blackfoot Agent, Edwin Aaron C. Hatch, who had shipped his annuities up the river on the *St. Mary* and then began transporting them via Mackinaw boat to the mouth of the Judith River, was himself three days ahead of the Mackeys and Culbertsons. Alfred J. Vaughan, agent for the Upper Missouri tribes since 1852, later wrote in his annual report for 1856 that "Nothing occurred to mar the pleasure of our trip except the loss of one of the employés of the 'American Fur Company,' who fell overboard and was drowned."[140]

At last the Mackeys and Culbertsons set out from fort Union by land, as summed up in Elkanah's Report:

[140] *Annual report of the Commissioner of Indian Affairs,* for the year 1856 Report No. 2, Fort Union, Sep 10, 1856, "My fourth annual report", Alfred J. Vaughan, published 1857. (JHT – I have found no other mention of this death.)

I will embrace the opportunity of giving you an abstract of what we have done since leaving Fort Union on the 26th of July.

Our journey from there to Fort Benton occupied us just three weeks. During this time we were dwellers in tents & never set foot in human habitation. Our way led us up the Missouri to the mouth of the Milk River, thence up Milk River until we passed the Bear's Paw Mountains & thence across a wide prairie until we reached the Missouri again at Fort Benton not far from the base of the Rocky Mountains.

Our company consisted of Alexander Culbertson, Esq. and his family, his cousin John Culbertson [141] from Cin. Ohio, S. A. Bennett, Esq. of St. Louis, and Mrs. Mackey & myself, besides the men who drove the teams & some 15 or 20 Assinaboin Indians who were going to smoke the pipe of peace with the Blackfeet. The trip was diversified with some pleasant & some rather unpleasant variety.

It was pleasant to see vast herds of Buffalos grazing on the prairie; and as we approached & saw them raise their heads, snuff the wind & bound away followed by our Indian hunters on fleet footed steeds, who were sure to return to our camp laden with the spoils, then it was exciting. The timid Elk more quick to detect our approach would lay his branching antlers back upon his shoulders and dash away, apparently proud of his own fleetness, and defying the hunter's pursuit. The antelope, full of curiosity, would come almost within rifle shot of us, and then skim away over the prairie as swift as the wind until he reached some eminence where he would stop & turn around to survey again the passing wonder.

These were some of the pleasant varieties.

---

[141] According to Jack Holterman this was John Purviance Culbertson, one of six children of Dr. Samuel (D.) Culbertson and Nancy Purviance. *King of the High Missouri*, p. 124.

The dismal howling of the wolves at night was not so pleasant, tho' we had no fear that they would enter our camp. We were detained two days on the banks of Poplar River until the flood would subside, that we might cross over, and one night our tent blew down and we were obliged to take refuge in Mr. Culbertson's and tie it fast to the wagons with ropes to prevent it from suffering a similar fate.

In the morning my hat was gone & after we scoured the prairie for some time, Mrs. Culbertson found it two miles from the camp. Mr. Bennett's, which was also gone, could not be found at all. These were not so unpleasant as they might have been. We laughed about them at the time, & now we find that they rather add than take away from the interest of a retrospect.

principally of the Gros Ventres
and Paeguns, on our way. They
all greeted us with a hearty welcome. Mrs. Mackey was to
them an object of great curiosity.
They had never seen a white
woman before, as no one
before her had ever been up
the Missouri higher than
the mouth of Milk River.
They treated her with the
greatest respect & kindness.

Facsimile from Elkanah's Report of section concerning Sarah's Reception among the Indians

We saw a good many Indians, principally of the Gros Ventres and Paeguns on our way. They all greeted us with a hearty welcome. Mrs. Mackey was to them an object of great curiosity. They had never seen a white woman before, as no one before her had ever been up the Missouri higher than the mouth of Milk River. They treated her with the greatest respect & kindness. [142]

But Sarah's Diary gives us a much more detailed account of that journey, and deserves to be given in full here:

Saturday, July 26th . We left Fort Union for Fort Benton about nine o'clock this morning. Our party consists of Mr. and Mrs. Culbertson and their little daughter, Fanny. Mr. John Culbertson, his cousin, Mr. Bennet, a young lawyer from St. Louis, Mr. Mackey & myself. Accompannied by Joe Ramsey [143] & his little son to hunt for us, Peepee [144] the driver of the baggage Cart & cook; Chouquette, the carriage driver and Akaisona [145] Mrs. Culbertson's servent boy. We started with four mules to the carriage, one horse with an ox before him to the baggage cart.

Mr. A. Culbertson riding on a mule. Mr. J. Culbertson & Mr. Bennet on horses. Mrs. Culbertson and Fanny, Mr. Mackey & myself in the carriage, Akaisona with Peepee in the baggage cart. Soon after leaving the Fort the baggage cart stalled, the ox would not pull up hill. We were obliged to send him back & get a horse in his place. We put two of our carriage mules before the horse in the cart, which left us only two to the carriage and Akaisona rides the fresh horse for the present.

---

[142] E. D. Mackey, Report, November 13, 1856

[143] Joseph Ramsey was a Mexican or Spaniard who had been a hunter for Fort Union since 1840. His Spanish name was Jose Ramuso or Ramisie. After he lost a hand through the bursting of his gun he looked after the horse herd at the fort. . . .in 1871 described as . . . a "tall good-looking old man of Spanish type. He spoke English very imperfectly. He was dressed like an Indian . . ." – Notes and References, *M. H. S. Contributions, Vol X.*

[144]Probably "Pepe, " Joseph Vasquez.

[145] I can find no other references to this young man. I don't believe Holterman mentions him. However his name may be spelled quite differently elsewhere.

We have come about twelve miles over a rough hilly road and have crossed the Little Muddy Creek & are encamped on its banks. My head aches violently.

Mr. Culbertson says they have always been in the habit of traviling on the Sab., but during the trip this time we will rest on that day.

Tomorrow, however we must travel as our camp is very much exposed to the sun & the musquitos are very bad.

Monday, July 28th. Yesterday we traveled twenty-seven miles & encamped on the east bank of the Big Muddy Creek, several miles above its mouth.

For the first eighteen or twenty miles our course lay through a beautiful vally, from two to four miles wide, leading us to the Missouri at its upper termination. This vally was very likely, at one time, the bed of the Missouri.

Peepee upset the baggage cart twice yesterday on the latter part of the road without dammage except the braking of some bottles which contained Nappeocke.[146]

Mr. Hollins, with two men returning to the Fort from where they built the Mackinaw boats, joined us & encamped for the night. This morning we were up bright & early so as to get the assistance of Mr. Hollins & party in crossing the Creek.

As there was a deep bed of mud in the bottom of the creek we unloaded our baggage & the men packed it over on their backs. Mr. Mackey, I & the driver got in the carriage to cross over, but the load being to heavy, the Mules stuck fast in the mud & to lighten it, the driver jumped in the stream & Joe Ramsy got Mr. Mackey on his back & carried him back to the bank. It was thought best for me to remain in the carriage. The men got at the wheels and the Mules flowndered through the mud till they got about the middle of the stream, there we stuck

---

[146] *Naapiaohkii* - a Blackfoot word for alcoholic spirits/ whiskey. www.blackfootdigitallibrary.com

fast & both the Mules got down. The men took out the mules, pulled the carriage through the stream them selves then tied a long rope to the tung & hitched the Mules to [it] and drew it up the bank & thus we got through at last. Mr. Mackey rode a Mule over & Joe Ramsy carried Mrs. Culbertson on his back. This all occurred before breakfast.

We pitched our tents there all day and let the horses rest.

But after breakfast we found the Musquitos so bad that we were obliged to decamp and proceed on our jorney. Before Hollins & party left, we exchanged a horse for a Mule. And put three Mules to the carriage & two Mules & one horse to the cart.

After proceeding seven or eight miles it came on a very severe rain storm & we stoped at a winter house belonging to the Fur company. [147] On our way the mules plunged into a sink hole and the carriage stuck fast, we had all to jump out and drag the carriage out of the mud. It continued raining till evening when it cleared off beautifully in time to dry the grass. Mr. Mackey pitched our tent as we prefered sleeping in the pure open air. The remainder of our company slept in the house. We all went out a fishing. Mr. Bennet caught several large fish which we will have for breakfast

Joe Ramsey & son left us at Big Muddy to return to the Fort. We are now obliged to depend on the resorces of our own party for game. Day before yesterday he shot us a duck & yesterday an Antilope which will last us for some days.

Tuesday, July 29th. We left our encampment early this morning, overtook the Mackinaw bots, soon after the middle of the day & encamped on the bank of the

---

[147] The geography indicates this may have been Fort Stewart, north of the Missouri river near the mouth of Big Muddy Creek, from 1855 - 1856, run by Frost, Todd & Co. Also (later) called Fort Kipp.

Missouria after a jorney of about seventeen miles through the prairie.

We passed some very paculiar looking sand banks with flat rocks on their tops. We have had to eat our fresh meat without any salt untill we got some from the boat today. The salt was forgotten when we left the Fort. We saw plenty of deer and Antilope and one old Buffalo which we did not consider worth shooting.

Wednesday, July 30th. We were on our way as early as possible this morning again. The morning being cool & clear we antisipated a long ride before us. But, when we reached the banks of Poplar River, after traveling about ten miles, we found the river so swollen by the recent rain we could not cross, and therefore were obliged to encamp & wait for it to fall.

Our jorney today has been over beautiful rolling prairie covered with short grass. Soon after leaving our encampment we met the hunters belonging to the boats who had caught a fine fat deer, which they gave us. After proceeding a few miles further we saw one of the finest sights we ever beheld, we were right in the midst of an abundance of Buffalo, and in every direction as far as we could see the hills and valleys were covered, thousands upon thousands were in sight, and their roaring sounded, & as we are here incamped we still hear it sounding like the mingled noise of distant thunder & the rattling of a thousand wagons over a stone pavement. Mr. Culbertson shot two of the roaming kind. He took out their tounges & left the rest there as they were old and tough. This evening John Culbertson & Chouquette shot a grizzly bear, it floted down the river and they could not get it out. A number of Antelope, Deer and Wolves are a1so visible.

Thursday, July 31st. The water continues high. The sun is setting behind a cloud. This morning our three horses were gone and Chouquette has been gone hunting them all day and returned without them. About

Mr. Bennet & one of the Indians cought several large catfish which still will make us a fine breakfast.

noon the wagons of the Opposition Company came up and encamped near us, to wait also for the falling of the river. Some Indians came in from the Assinaboin camp, wh. is on the Poplar several miles above us. They assure us that none of their nation took the horses. Several of them are going with us when we move on, in order to meet some of the Blackfeet & settle the preliminaries for a permanent peace. Tobacco has been exchanged between them.

Friday, August 1st. Last night we had a terrible blow, it came on about midnight. Our tent blew down on top of us. We crept out from under it the best way we could. I got the quilt around me & we made our way to Mr. Culbertson's tent which was still standing. The men drew the carriage around and fastened the tent to it with ropes. Mr. Mackey drove some pins in ours to keep it from blowing clear off. We remained in Mr. C.'s till morning, when we got our own erected again.

Mr. Mackey could not find his hat & concluded the wind must have blowen it away. Mr. Bennet knew that his had blown away, for it blew off his head in the night. Mrs. Culbertson found Mr. Mackey's more than a mile from the camp. Mr. Bennet could not find his. He has been rather unfortunate since we left Fort Union, he has lost his whip, his horse and hat, however he got an old hat which Mr. Culbertson chanced to have along, which answers the purpose.

Chouquette returned at noon again without the horses. The water had fallen then so that we could cross & we were obliged to proceede on our journey with our six mules, with three to the carriage and three to the cart. We got across very well, met Major Hatch & Mr. Dawson on the other side of the river. They came from the boats to see how we were getting on. We [went/count] about eight miles this afternoon &

encamped on the banks of the Missouri. The Opposition Company went further to encamp.

Monday, August 4th. I sprained my foot on Sat. morning, just before we left our encampment. We had two Mules to the carriage & two to the cart & took the other two to ride. But there was still one a wanting so all the gentlemen took a turn at walking.

It was a long, long day to me, I gave many a long look for the camping ground. We traveled about twenty five miles. The pain of my foot was very great. When we got to our encampment they had to carry me from the carriage to the tent. Mr. Mackey did everything in his power to relieve me.

After baithing it a few times & keeping it perfectly still the pain was not so great. On Sabbath morning it was much better, but I could not use it at all. I was in great hope that they would rest but Mr. Culbertson said they would have to travvell, but after that we got to Milk River we could stop whenever we chose.

He said we would leave early in the morning and get to our encampment early and we could have religious servis. We did start early & travaled all day long till late in the evening. The mules were fairly given out & we went along very slow. We encamped on the Porcupine fork of Milk River. My foot did not pain me so, but was very helples, I was obliged to keep it very still on a pillow. I was very weary before reaching our encampment.

Just as Mr. Culbertson reached it on Mule back, he met some men bringing us a fresh supply of mules and horses from Fort Benton, which he had sent on for when we reached Fort Union. We were yet more than half a mile behind & one of our mules so near given out that we had to stop every few rods. Mr. Culbertson sent a man with a fresh mule to meet us. Against [the time] we got our tents up & something to eat, it was very late and we were all very tired and serves had to be dispensed with. We had two bad crossings during the day, one at Porcupine Creek & the other, which was <u>very</u> bad, at another little stream which has no name.

In going up the hill one of the mules would not pull but lay down on the tongue & broke it off. They were all out of the carriage but me, I had to sit there till they lifted me out & stay where they lifted me till they lifted me in again. We saw a great many buffalo today. The Indians shot several fine buffalo cows.

We left our encampment early this morning with [?5] fresh mules & two horses, this furnished us with three to the carriage, the same number to the cart, one apiece for the riders, one to pack the meat on & the one that gave out runs idle. We came about eighteen miles & are encamped on the bank of Milk river.

We have had a very pleasant cool day & a very pleasant ride although part of it was over a very rough rode and we had a bad crossing at the Porcupine Fork. But got along well & encamped early. Mr. Mackey, Mr. Bennet and Mr. J. Culbertson have gone a fishing. Mr. Bennet & Mr. Culbertson have just returned, and Mr. Bennet has one fish & says Mr. Mackey has caught one & is trying [to] get another that bit his hook off. I was able, with Mr. Mackey's help to walk or rather limp to breakfast this morning for the first since I got my foot hurt. Mr. Mackey has now returned with two fish but not the one that bit off his hook. Mr. A. Culbertson shot a buffalo cow this evening, just above our tent.

Tuesday, August 5th. Our camp this evening is in a beautiful Cottonwood grove by a large pond of water some distance from Milk River. We have come about twenty miles today over rather a rough road, some times on a high prairie & sometimes on a low bottom. One place we passed by looked as though there had been a stone wall built to keep the high prairie from falling down into the bottom, but it had apparently fallen over. The cherries are now ripe & we get some to eat every day.

We came to one very bad crossing on one little stream of water. The men made a willow bridge to cross on. We had all to alight from the carriage till they got it over. As my foot is still weak from the sprain, Mr. Mackey and Mr. Culbertson had to pack me over, as they call it, out in this country.

Wednesday, August 6th. This evening we have crossed Trappers Fork of Milk River & are encamped on its banks. We crossed about noon. In the evening, about Sundown, the waggons of the Opposition Company came up & crossed. We have not seen anything of them before since we passed them Saturday about noon. Major Hatch & his man from the Mackinaw boats came up with them. And intend to proceede on in company with us to Fort Benton.

We had two bad crossings today -- one over a small stream soon after we started and the other over Trappers' Fork. At the first the men made a willow bridge. Mr. Mackey & Mr. Culbertson packed me over. At the second, the Mules in the cart mired and they had to take them from the cart & pull it out by hand. The Indians who are along laid their sholders to & helped to pull. Just before we reached Trapper's Fork, quite an exciting scene occurred.

A Blackfoot Indian, who had come down from Fort Benton with the fresh supply of horses & mules, rode down through the prairie & started after some Buffalo. He singled out a big *stomik* [148] & gave chase to him. He came right towards us under full run -- passed just in front of our mules & coming to a deep or rather high embankment over which he feared to plunge, he wheeled short to the left & went full drive towards the mule on which the Dutchman, Jake,[149] who had also come down from Fort Benton, was riding. The mule was frightened almost as much as the Buffalo but mule like would not run. He stopped stalk still and kicked up with both feet into the Buffalo's face at the same time

[148] Blackfoot word for bison/buffalo.

[149] Probably Jacob Schmidt, born in Germany, trained as a tailor, who worked at Fort Benton for Andrew Dawson from 1854-1863.

throwing the Dutchman over his head. We were frightened, expecting the mule or the Buffalo, or both, to run over him, but the mule stood still, the Buffalo turned to the left & ran on & the Dutchman got up not at all hurt by the fall but raving at the Indian for thus endangering his life. When we saw he was not hurt we could not refrain from a hearty laugh. The Indian, nothing daunted, continued his pursuit but did not shoot the Buffalo. His revolver was out of order & would not go off when he got in shooting distance.

The Mackeys had not complained much since the first few days, but Joel Overholser quoted a traveler (possibly Agent Hatch) who came from the Milk River to Fort Benton in 1856, and found the "misquitoes frightful".[150]

As Sarah wrote, the overland party met Blackfoot Agent Hatch on July 29th and again on Aug 1st and 6th, when he joined their overland expedition. He seems to have been traveling in the mackinaw Sarah mentions. According to the Agent's own journal entry for the 29th : "Met Culbertson and party: Mackeys with him 'The first white woman in the country'."[151] This was near the mouth of the Poplar river where they were delayed two days by flood waters.

Agent Hatch was bringing up annuities for distribution in September at the mouth of the Judith. Hatch's Journal does not mention the Culbertsons or Mackeys again until mid-August.

---

150 "Tourist Attractions 1856," Joel F. Overholser, *River Press*, 29 July 1981.

151 from Edwin Hatch's Journal in appendix concerning Mackeys in *Montana Historical Society Contributions*, Vol X, "Notes and References," p. 279 (hereafter *M. H. S. Contributions, Vol X*)
Note: Joseph La Barge's wife, Pélagie, who came up to Fort Union on the boat *Martha* in 1847/8, is spoken of as the first white woman on the Upper Missouri. See Holterman, p. 79.

Although it was not written until a month later, it is appropriate to consider Lowrie's answer to two of Elkanah's letters here.[152]

> Rev. E. D. Mackey
> My Dear Sir,
>
> (We have received your) letter of 4 June (sent from) Bellevue (& of 22 July, [postmarked] from) Fort Union. We were glad to hear (you arrived safe & sound at that ?head). (Also) your (last letter, so thus) the good providence(?) of God has (passed) you safely (onward) to your mountains & Indians – You need have had no uneasiness about the purchase of the mattress & bedding, for you will have need of them at the mission.
>
> I am very sorry that you did not get your boxes at Iowa Point. She [153] had I understood passed there in the night. The boxes were at the nearest store(?) just to the left(?) of the bank(?). I have written to have them sent to a(?) missionary where they will be taken care of.
>
> The mail to Fort Pierre from Sioux City(?) is carried on horseback, and they dislike and often refuse to carry newspapers and pamphlets. I wrote to Dr. Wm. Moffett on the subject, and he kindly offered to take charge of any letters and papers we might send to you through him. He fears the papers will not go regularly, but says he will forward them by the earliest opportunity (ies?). I regret much that you will be so deprived of the current (press?). I will however send to Dr. Moffett's care *The Home and Foreign Record, The Foreign Missionary* and *the Presbyterian*, and next spring when the Boat goes up, a good supply. Let us hope the

---

[152] Apparently Elkanah did not receive this letter. He complains of no letters from Lowrie in his "Private Letter" of November 5, 1856. "I hoped to hear from you at Ft. Pierre in reference to the Gov. appropriation & c. but not a line nor a paper nor a periodical did we get from New York . . ."
NOTE: The queries in parentheses indicate illegibility.
[153] "She," the steamboat.

means of communication will(?) become better every year.

(We?) shall be glad if Mr. Jenkinson will consent (to join?) you next spring. We hoped before this time (that we?) would have learned(?) what the Department (would?) have(?) agreed to do in aid of the Blackfeet (school?). But the appropriation was not made (so?) near the close of the session, and as soon as (?) Congress adjourned, the Commissioner of Indian Affairs had to leave to visit some Indian tribes in the North, and he has not yet returned. We cannot therefore know what the Govt. will do, in time for the October express from Fort Pierre.

The Committee therefore have to act on their own ability, and in reference to their own funds, till we know what the Department will do. They have agreed therefore to send one other mission family, Mr. Jenkinson if he will go, and also furnish you with funds, to put up suitable buildings for yourselves, to an amount not exceeding four(?) thousand dollars. Provided, however that your letters do not discourage us from sending another family. Should the Department give us a liberal stipend(?) for a boarding school, then of course we shall change(?) the number, and enlarge the means for building but till we know what we(?) shall(?) receive, and till we(?) hear from you we think(?) (it) best not to commend the building of a boarding school, till we have(?) further light. We would have been glad to have been able to(?) have written at once in regard of the boarding school, but we have no more light now than when you left.

...After all our plans for the private (?) buildings, and after I had sent up from St. Louis 600 (?) lbs of lime, the workmen (?) there found they could not build of concrete. The stone was difficult to be got, and very hard to break, and they had to haul the sand a good distance. They therefore decided to build of stone. Mr. Jenkinson therefore will get no experience of that kind of building there. Nor do I suppose you could easily get the materials for that kind of building at Fort Benton. But on this point we shall hear from you in due time.

We are all going on here in the usual way. In the community generally there is a good deal of excitement in regard to the presidential election. The friends of Buchanan & Fremont are both sanguine of their success. Filmore's[154] friends also express a hope of his election. In Kansas there has been much excitement, and what is worse, some bloodshed on both sides. The friends of peace are in hopes that the new governor [155] will be able to put a stop, at least to the fighting, but he has a very difficult position to occupy.

You are not forgotten here, & we find (?) many prayers daily ascend to heaven on your behalf. Your letter from Fort Union was published, and has been read with interest.

That every blessing may rest upon you is my earnest prayer, & with best wishes I am affectionately yours,

Walter Lowrie[156]

Sarah's Diary, describing the last week of the overland trip from Fort Union to Fort Benton, from the Milk River, makes it sound as though things weren't nearly as difficult as the first part of the trip:

Thursday, Aug. 7th. We are encamped this evening on the south side of Milk River, having crossed

---

[154] Millard Fillmore, vice president under Zachary Taylor, became the 13th president, assuming the office after Taylor's death in 1850. He refused to join the emerging Republican Party in 1856, but ran for the presidency under the banner of the American Party, which was affiliated with the Know-Nothing movement.,

[155] John W. Geary, appointed governor of Kansas Territory On July 31, 1856. He resigned March 12, 1857, leaving at night to escape assassination by members of his political party. Later a Major General in the Union Army and Governor of Pennsylvania.

[156] Walter Lowrie, LTR, to E. D. Mackey, September (?15 or 16) 1856.

it about ten o'clock this morning. We did not travel more than five or six miles today as it would have been too long a journey to have gone to the next good camping place. They had to construct a willow bridg to cross Milk River. We got across without much trouble. Mr. Mackey went a swimming with Mr. Bennet and J. Culbertson this afternoon, he swam across Milk River several times.

Milk River near Junction of Missouri, lithograph by John Mix Stanley. ca 1855

Friday, Aug. 8th. We started across the prairie this morning & after travelling 10 or 12 miles struck the river again and encamped. Just before encamping came by where the Grosventies of the Prairie had once had a Medicine lodge. This evening the wind is blowing pretty hard. John Culbertson, Mr. Bennet and Mr. Mackey went about two miles to a small creek across the river where Akaisona said very large turtles were to be found as large as he could reach around, with necks as long as his arm. They went right after dinner & when they got there they were informed that they would have to wait until the sun went down & then the turtles would come up. They concluded that it was not advisable to wait.

Sat., Aug. 9th. Our camp this evening is at the head of the grande detour or big bend of Milk River. We struck across the prairie & came a journey of about 18 miles. Major Hatch shot a large rattlesnake with 9 rattles. A few miles up the River, above where we encamped last night, is a large stone resembling a buffalo lying down. John Culbertson and Mr. Bennet, led by Akaisona, came by it this morning and say it is quite a curiosity. John found a stone very much resembling a petrified Duck egg.

Monday, August 11th. Another excuse for travelling yesterday. We were almost out of provisions & we must get on where there was Buffalo. We stopped to rest a short time at noon and travelled until late in the evening. Strange that our Sabbath day's journey is always the longest. We crossed Milk River again & had one bad place where the bluffs came very near the river.

Today we have had another long journey. We want to reach the Fort on Sat. We saw several bands of Antelope and Elk, but no Buffalo. Our hunter killed an Antelope. Our camp this evening is in a beautiful spot on the north side of Milk River. Yesterday & today we have been in sight of the Bear's Paw. The flat prairies, through wh. we have come today are very barren, in some places entirely bare, in others covered with the Cactus & wild sage.

Tuesday, August 12th. Our Camp this evening is on Milk River, seven miles below our last crossing. We have come twenty five or thirty miles to day. There is no water in the river here at all except where it stands in holes and was none where we camped last night except in holes. We crossed the Two Forks to day, stoped for dinner after crossing the Second. These were as dry as the main Stream. It was remarked that the cows must have gone dry.

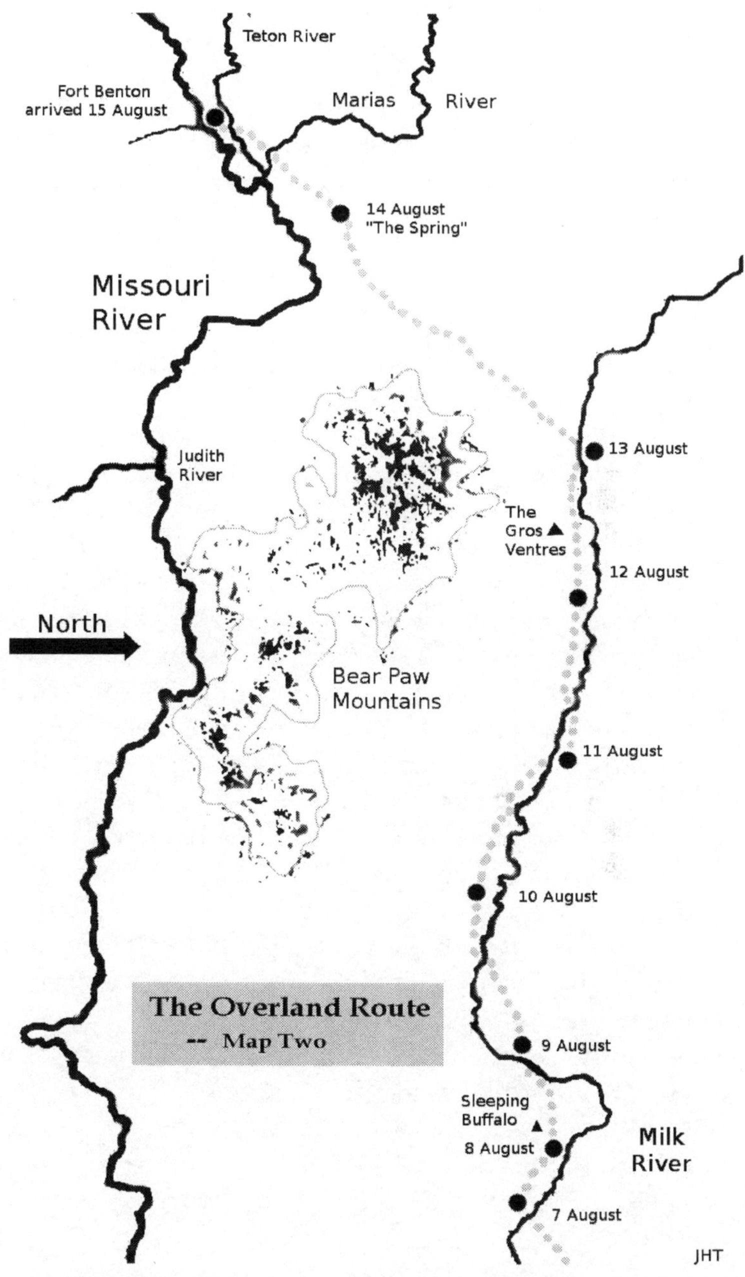

Traces of Indians were discovered in the forenoon & early in the afternoon we came to a place where they had been encamped lately but have not seen any of them yet. We followed their trail this afternoon and will probably over take them in a day or two. A whip was found, which Mrs. Culbertson says shows by its construction that they are Grosventres. Mrs. C. fears lest the Blackfeet or Grosventres attack the Assinaboins who are with us. It is now raining some & blowing quite hard.

Wednesday, Aug. 13th. We struck our tents early this morning & were soon on our way. Major Hatch & his man left us & rode on towards the Fort as they could travel faster than we. Soon after crossing the River seven miles above our camp we saw some Indians at a distance on the hill & presently about 12 or 15 Gros Ventres came over the hill on prancing steeds & galloped toward us. Of the Assinaboins who were with us, two were on horseback & the rest afoot . When the Gros Ventres came within about fifty yards of us, one of the Assinaboins galloped towards them. Mrs. Culbertson felt excited fearing a collision & jumped out of the carriage, but her fears proved groundless. They met the Assinaboin in a friendly manner, he turned his horse and they all rode together to meet us.

After friendly greetings were over and the Assinaboins had entertained the Gros Ventres with a song, they all sat down on the prairie, the A's to dress & paint their faces, and the G's to get ready their sacred pipes. They had four of these done up with a great deal of care in three or four different wrappers. They were carefully ornamented with feathers, horse hair, beads, etc. They unrolled them here but smoked only their common pipes. We then proceeded about a mile farther & they all sat down again to smoke. By this time we had perhaps one hundred Gros Ventres with us, including their chief.

We then went on about a mile farther & came to their camp, went into a large lodge and the common pipes were passed around several times while the sacred ones were getting ready. The stem of one of them seemed to be stopped up on this occasion. The other three were lighted by those who had charge of them & after some manouvres were gone through with them, they were handed to the chief to smoke & one of them to Mr. Culbertson also, who sat by his side. They were then carefully rolled up & put away. These pipes are smoked only on great occasions when a peace is to be made & then the tobacco is used, wh. had been exchanged when proposals of peace were made.

We left the A's with the G's to transact the rest of the matter themselves & stopped for dinner a short distance from the Camp. Quite a number of the Indians - men, women, and children, came down to see us -- I was quite an object of curiosity. They had never seen a white woman before as no one has ever been up in this country higher than the Mouth of Milk River. The women & children seemed most curious then, but this evening 15 or 20 men came to our camp wh. is 8 or 10 miles from theirs on the Little Beaver Creek. They collected around the front of our tent & stood gazing at me for near an hour. They are altogether friendly disposed & kind.

We started after dinner, about one o'clock, & on our way hither passed within two or three miles of the Paegun camp. Quite a number of them rode out to meet us & several times we had to stop & talk with them. They are a band of Blackfeet. Two of their principal men came out. Mr. C. gave all who came small presents of tobacco, sugar, etc. When one of the principal men was informed of the object for wh. we came, he gave us the right hand of friendship.

A Paegun, who had been a prisoner among the Crows returned home with us. His friends received him with great joy, even wept for joy & gave him a horse & three blankets to ride on. The Blackfeet & Gros Ventres have all a great number of fine horses. This tribe is called Grosventres of the Prairie to distinguish them from the Grosventres of the Missouri.

Thursday, Aug. 14th. Today we had a very long trip of about 45 miles across the prairie. Took dinner on the River Sans Bois = the woodless river. [157] We met many Indians on the way and were hailed by all with friendly greetings. Just after sunset we reached "The Spring" with mules & horses & people all tired & thirsty, but what was our disappointment to find that the spring contained no water. Not a drop to be seen. After digging a hole in the sand where the spring was wont to be, we got enough of muddy water to quench our thirst and make some coffee, but very little for the animals. Supped after dark, without a candle, on jerked buffalo meat & coffee. About midnight the wagons of the Opposition Company came up & encamped near us.

Friday, Aug. 15th. Started early & went to the Marias River before breakfast, a distance of 8 or 10 miles. We all united in saying the Maria was one of the prettiest streams we had ever seen, A clear mountain stream -- every pebble distinctly visible at the bottom. Both ourselves & our animals were glad to drink freely of it and slake our thirst after so long an abstinence. After breakfast we got washed & dressed for the great event of entering the Fort. Some of Mrs. Culbertson's Indian friends came out all the way to the Maria, 12 miles, to meet her. [continued below]

On August 15, the Fort Benton *Journal* notes, "This day Mr. Culbertson and party arrived, the opposition people arrive also . . ."[158]

For his part, Agent Hatch recorded on the 15th, "Culbertson party reached Benton," and on the next day, he wrote, "The Priest and his wife appear to be pleased

---

[157] Can't find other references to River San Bois – may be either Boxelder or Big Sandy Creeks.

[158] M. H. S. Contributions, Vol X, Fort Benton *Journal*

with the place, Indians and country - will probably get enough of it before spring."[159]

The appearance of the Fort, though recently under construction, must have been somewhat disorderly. It had originally been built entirely of wood in 1847-8, with wooden palisades, but partly out of his experience at Ft. Laramie, Alexander Culbertson had decided to make an adobe fort and began the work in 1850:

> . . .Since the fall of 1850 was a warm one, it was quite right for the manufacture of adobes, which were made and sun-dried on the spot and nick-named "doughboys" . . .by the engages. They were . . .about 6 x 4 x 15 inches in size, . . .Progress continued until Alec's own residence of two stories was completed, shortly before Christmas, 1850. It would take another decade to rebuild the rest of the fort. Evidently the log structures were replaced by adobe walls little by little with some of the original log walls retained.[160]

How much of it was completed at that stage is unclear, but during the previous three months, the Fort Benton Journal reported the manufacture of "doughboys" or "dubbies," that is "adobes". These adobe bricks were made of mud and grass, with "burned lime" in the bricks and/or the mortar. The men were making more than eleven hundred of them a day at the peak of manufacture.

Then in late June, using the adobes, they started the construction of a high "bastion" using scaffolding. This seems to have been the "blockhouse" nearest the river which still stands as part of the refurbished Fort Benton in the Montana town of that name. Charcoal was being made and brought from the Teton river valley nearby,

---

[159] M. H. S. Contributions, Vol X Agent Hatch's Diary

[160] Holterman, *King of the High Missouri*, p. 89

possibly for slaking the lime, or baking the "dobies," but also for blacksmith work. The roofing of the Bastion was starting by the carpenters as of June 18.[161]

And on August 12, the acting factor had the fort whitewashed.

So despite the disorder, the Fort must have looked impressive, while the smell of fresh adobe and sawdust mingled with the familiar smell of the river, must have been among the impressions that greeted the Mackeys and Culbertsons on their arrival 15 August.

Sarah's Diary makes it sound almost idyllic:

John Mix Stanley's depiction of Fort Benton in 1853

> [*15 Aug* continued] We reached the Fort about two o'clock, amidst the firing of cannon in honor of Mr. Culbertson's arrival. It is in a beautiful spot on the left bank of the Missouri whose waters at this point are as

---

[161] M. H. S. Contributions, Vol X Fort Benton Journal, pp 74-84 Note, however, that the carpenters were still at work on the Bastion as of September 4, so Mrs. Mackey must have experienced that noise, at least until they finished the roof on the 6th.

> clear as if they had just gushed "from their fountains in the mountains."[162]
>
> The bluffs both above and below come close to the river & then the bottom widening out on both sides of the river forms a beautiful amphitheatre inclosed by high bluffs & containing an area of perhaps 2 or 3 thousand acres. Back of the Fort a bluff stands out by itself and the low prairie extends clear around it. The Fort is built of Adobe about 200 ft. square and has two story houses, one room deep nearly all around it. The windows all look towards the inside of the Fort and the back walls of the houses form the walls of the Fort.

This is the last of Sarah's own diary entries.

Despite her light-hearted records, we learn from Elkanah's Report that she, from early on in the trip, had been experiencing another sort of "unpleasant diversion" than those noted during their cross-country camping trip:

> The trip across the country would doubtless have been invigorating to her as it was to me had it not been for her previous delicate state of health. But as it was it proved too much for her, she was sick a good deal on the way, but through the merciful care of a tender Father she was enabled to perform the journey.

Sarah must have been putting on a brave face toward others, but according to her husband's Report:

> Two days after we reached Fort Benton she was taken down & continued very weak and nervous up to the time of Mr. Culbertson's leaving the Fort to return . . .

---

[162] Possibly a reference to lines from "The Cataract At Lodore" by Robert Southey: "From its fountains in the mountains . . ."

Elkanah wrote nearly a month later in his journal, taking up where Sarah's diary left off:

> *Friday, September 12th.* Four weeks ago to-day we reached Fort Benton. The second day after our arrival Mrs. M. was taken sick - confined to bed for one week and to her room for nearly two. She then recovered so much as to be able to walk out, but remained, & still remains, very weak & in a distressing state of nervous derangement, unable to sleep at night, harrassed with frightful visions, dread of impending evils & anticipations of approaching calamities. These things taken in connection with the fact that she is looking forward to the epoch, justly dreaded by all women even under the most favorable circumstances and that here <u>no one</u> could be obtained to render her <u>any assistance</u> at that difficult & trying time, have led us to consider the question of returning home.

Fort Benton, with the "Bastion" in the foreground, as seen from the bank of the Missouri

Despite Sarah's illness and these concerns, Elkanah continued with his hand on the plow. Two days later, on that first Sunday after their arrival, he held services.

The Fort Benton Journal tells us, ". . .We had a sermon from the Rev. Mr. Mackey in Mr. C.'s room and one in the Indian House for the Indians."[163] And Agent Hatch recorded:

> *Aug 17, 1856* Today probably for the first time the walls of Fort Benton echoed to the sound of Protestant divine services. Not a very numerous audience but very attentive. I did not attend. [164]

On the next day, Agent Hatch noted the poor health of two persons: "Mrs. Mackey and Mr. Culbertson both unwell."[165] That brief statement might lead one to think some flu, or communicable disease, perhaps food poisoning was doing the rounds. A few days earlier the overland party had drunk from the brackish "spring". However, it becomes clear Sarah Mackey was suffering from a condition not communicable, one that Alexander Culbertson, for all his accomplishments, could not share.

In the days that followed, Agent Hatch made several other references to the Mackeys:

> *Aug. 20, 1856* Mrs. Mackey some better and they talk of going down again this fall.
>
> *Aug. 31, 1856* Preaching up stairs
>
> *Sept. 1, 1856* Mr. Mackey started for the falls with Chouquette.

---

163 M. H. S. Contributions, Vol X Fort Benton *Journal*

164 ibid.

165 ibid.

> *Sept 7, 1856* Mr. Mackey did not preach today. . . .Why? I do not know.[166]

Elkanah's *Report* mentions preaching every Sabbath at Fort Benton,[167] leaving Hatch's last entry as one more minor mystery. Perhaps Elkanah preached too quietly for those not in attendance to hear. Or possibly he preached at the "opposition fort," Fort Campbell.

A gap in the Fort Benton *Journal* for three weeks from August 18 to September 2, seems to be explained by the next entry:

> *Wed. 3* – A. Rose[168] returned after an absence of fifteen days found the Blood Indians and Blackfeet Camps and deld [delivered] the Words of the Agent – Mr. Culbertson this day started for the boats with the Mule and four pack animals.[169]

It appears Alexander Rose was the keeper of the *Journal* at the fur post. [170]

Alexander Culbertson was one of he overseers of the business of the fur company – going back and forth to get the rest of the freight up to the fort. This seems to be done by wagon, and by pack animals, overland, and by the small boats. The freight had been brought upriver

---

166 ibid.

167 E. D. Mackey, Report, November 13, 1856

168 Alexander Rose

169 M. H. S. Contributions, Vol X, Fort Benton *Journal*

170 ibid, MHS vol X, p259 – "When Major John Owen visited Fort Benton. July 1, 1856, Rose was in charge. .. .Rose kept the Fort Benton Journal from May 12 to October 17, 1856, and his entries show him to have had an average education for that time. Since there is no mention of him in the poll lists of 1864 he had either died or left the country prior to that date."

from Fort Union as far as possible by the steamboat[171], then, possibly in stages by the smaller boats to where it was variously loaded and carried overland. Culbertson seems to have done the oversight himself. According to the Fort Benton *Journal*, the wagon work was completed on 9 September, but the small boats did not arrive back at the Fort until October 11.[172]

Meanwhile, with Charles Chouquette[173] as his guide, Elkanah went exploring or perhaps we should say surveying around the country within thirty or forty miles of Fort Benton, particularly to the south.

Charles Chouquette was born at St. Charles, Missouri, in 1823. At 21 (1844) he was an employee of Pierre Chouteau, and in charge of a keelboat crew going upriver to Fort Union, which trip took 72 days. He seems to have worked on the Upper Missouri for the rest of his life. In April 1849, on his first trip higher on the river, he met Jim Bridger and about 80 other trappers just in time to fight the battle already alluded to, with a large party of Blackfoot warriors near Great Falls. On that same trip he helped move stores from Fort William to Fort Benton.

He married an Indian woman, Rosa Lee, in 1854, Father De Smet performing the ceremony. Charles was interpreter at the Stevens Treaty Council in 1855, and came up with Agent Hatch in 1856 as his interpreter. The 1870 census shows that he was a blacksmith and had a wife "Valerie", with five children 3 to 13 (oldest born about 1857). He built the first house in Fort Benton and worked there for T.C. Power. He moved his family to Old Agency (in what is now the Flathead Reservation) and is said to

---

171 about ninety miles above Fort Union: see text for footnote 49, under date July 12

172 M. H. S. Contributions, Vol X, Fort Benton *Journal*

173 We know the identity of his guide only through Hatch's September 1 entry above.

have built the first home there, in 1871. Still an employee of T. C. Power, he worked as a freighter among other things. In 1889 he moved to the Blackfoot Agency.

His children received their educations in the Midwest. One, Melinda, went to a St. Louis convent school. She married to John Wren, who worked for traders in Fort Benton. She died in Browning in 1940. [174]

Just prior to the arrival of the Culbertsons and Mackeys at Fort Union, Charles Chouquette had been about other American Fur business. We learn something of that life from the Fort Sarpy (a Yellowstone post) Journal kept by James H. Chambers. [175] In early June he and Chouquette had been working with J. F. Wray, and parting from Wray, set out to find some horses that had been lost or stolen. After three days of this, they only succeeded in having the rest of their horses stolen in the night. Chambers had a serious infection in his hand as they returned and came to a flooding river they had to cross. His accounts of June 6 and 7 read like this:

> Very sore this morning my right hand severely poisoned, noon'd at Frenchmans, came on to Big Muddy found it very high, kill'd a deer took the skin & tied up our clothes guns & blankets. Started across the Muddy had got but a few feet when the cramp took me in my left arm – being an expert swimmer I paid but little attention to it – I told Chouquette to keep on with the pack & I would make the shore. Some way when he got in the middle of the stream the cramp took me in the legs I went down twice, on coming up I laid my left arm

---

[174] Sources: *MHS Contributions*, Vol X, pp 277-8, and "Charles Chouquette Survived Hardships, Indian Battles" by Joel Overholser, *The River Press*, Wednesday Sept 9, 1981.

[175] Fort Sarpy Journal, *MHS Contributions*, Vol X, pp.100-187, edited by Mrs. Anne McDonnell, assistant librarian.

> on the pack & it turned over & fill'd. I told C- to keep on with the pack & I would manage to get over — he became frightened & let go of the pack which sunk to the bottom — I came near drowning but thank Providence I got out safe but perfectly naked & barefooted, forty seven miles of hard travelling before me the country full of Prickly Pears & Enemies nothing to protect my feet nor even a knife to defend myself — Chouquette dive & brot up a shirt & pr of pants — he got satisfied & left. Mosquitoes & horse flies very bad — I started at a trot & kept on untill ten O clock — the night very cool, Chouquette gave out — we laid down in the prairie — not to sleep but to shiver with the cold — made sixty five miles
>
> Sat. 7 — got up at day break very cold & stiff, Started C's teeth chattering like castanets, he begged of me to stop untill the sun would get up. I consented knowing well what I would suffer from the sun as I was entirely naked & he had shoes — pants & shirt, started when the sun got up & came slow — got to Little Muddy about 10 a.m., laid down in the willows for a couple of hours, could not stand the mosquitoes. Started C ahead to the Fort to send clothing to me, kept on & met Mr. R. Denig with a my horse & a suit of clothes one mile from the fort, arrived at 1 p. m. horribly sun burnt — made 17 miles.

Chambers was footsore and sun-burned from his nude promenade, and took more than a week to recover. meanwhile, on the 17th, Chouquette and another trader went back and recovered as much of Chamber's lost equipage as possible. On 17 June he wrote:

> Doing nothing of consequence Bouchie & Chouquette returned from the Big Muddy bring my rifle &c that I

> lost on the sixth ult — all right that accounts for the stains in this book being as it was one of drowned articles. I have not wrote up my journal on acount of my being buisy in the meantime ten Assynaboins have been kill'd by the Sioux — Sir Geo Gore arrived from a two years hunt, both company's boats arrived — A Missionary Doct Macky & Lady came to convert the Indians.

Although we have few details of Elkanah and Chouquette's trip, it sounds as though they may have ranged up Shonkin Creek into the Highwood Mountains, and across or along the mountains, then down Highwood or Belt Creek to the Missouri. They may have ascended the Missouri to the Great Falls and Giant Springs, said to be the largest freshwater spring in the world. Elkanah speaks of the Highwoods, but does not mention other natural spectacles in his Report. He does mention going west and north of Fort Benton into the Teton and Maria [Marias] River valleys.

The Marias River, from a lithograph by John Mix Stanley

The object of Elkanah's travels was finding a site for his mission, and particularly his boarding school, according to his Report:

> *The Site of a mission. Cost of building* & c. -- As the people have no local habitation, but wander over their country & pitch their tents wherever fancy and the pursuit of the Buffalo calls them, it will of course be impossible to carry on a dayschool. Any thing that is done for the present at least, to educate the children must be done in a boarding school. And as the great mass of their country is now & must, from present appearances, always remain utterly unfit for cultivation, one of the main questions in settling upon a location will be where can good tillable land be found convenient to timber & water?
>
> After all the information I have been able to obtain from personal exploration & inquiry I am prepared to recommend as the most eligible situation some point in the valley of the Highwood. This is a beautiful little stream rising in the Highwood mountains, some 30 miles South West from Fort Benton flowing thence Northward and emptying into the Missouri about 20 miles above the Fort, and a few miles below the falls. I obtained a guide & interpreter, was gone two days from the Fort & explored this valley from the mountains down almost to the river. At its head in the mountains pine can be obtained suitable for building purposes. Going downward, the valley for about 12 miles is from a quarter to half mile wide. The soil is loose, black & fertile, covered with luxuriant growth of grass & weeds. The "Bitter Cottonwood" grows all along near to the stream, in some cases widening out a little but in no case covering the whole bottom. Here [about 12 miles from the top] the bluffs come very near together, leaving just room enough for the stream to wind between them for about a mile. There again the valley opens out very much like that described above.

> At this point a dam could be built at very little expense, which might be used for driving a mill & also to irrigate the valley in case it should be needed. There are several good springs at different points & the stream is full of speckled trout.
>
> I visited also the valley of the Maria, and the Teton and passed along the Teton for several miles. In both these valleys there is a growth of cottonwood. The streams are beautiful & clear heading in the Rocky Mountains & flowing over a pebble bottom, but the soil is barren. [176]

Having noted the abundance of pine and cottonwood for lumber, Elkanah went on to discuss the construction of the mission buildings:

> If the Board would prefer to purchase buildings already erected, Fort Benton can be obtained from the American Fur Company & Mr. Culbertson is of the opinion that the land on the Missouri at that point is productive. In regard to the cost of building it is hard to make any very accurate estimate. There are no white men in the country but those in the employ of the Fur Companies. They hire their men in St. Louis & take them up to do their work. They pay common laborers about twenty dollars a month & tradesmen more. Twelve men in a year could probably put up a building of the smaller dimensions you gave me & their wages, the cost of getting them to the country & back and of boarding them while there would be the cost of the building. We would have nothing to pay for clay to make adobes & nothing for pine and cottonwood trees to make lumber. At a rough estimate I would say that such a building would cost not much short of ten thousand dollars.[177]

---

[176] ibid.

[177] ibid.

So Elkanah was even considering buying the fort itself for his school. Elkanah's Report also discusses aspects of running a mission school, addressing himself to the questions the Board asked him to consider:

> III. *The Article of Clothing* The children will want nothing better than the native moccasins so far as clothing for feet is concerned. They are a great deal more comfortable than our tight fashionable shoes & boots, made not to fit the foot, but Chinese like, to mould the feet into a supposed genteel shape. A part of their outer garments for the winter can be made from skins.
>
> IV *The article of bedding* This can be supplied chiefly by the use of Buffalo Robes.
>
> V. *Food for the children* The meat of the Buffalo is their principal food. This may be supplemented by vegetable food raise on the mission farm, so that there will be no necessity for taking up much food for them from St. Louis. –

Blackfoot Treaty Council, 1855, by Gustavus Sohon

> VI. Respecting female help We may be able to get some assistance from some of the Blackfeet women who have been about the forts & partly civilized. There are two women at Fort Benton, one of whom did some washing for us while we were there. These might be obtained to work at the Mission but I think very little dependence is to be placed upon help from that quarter.[178]

All of which indicates Elkanah was serious in his intention to bring the mission school into being, but had gained little familiarity or respect for the people he intended to teach.

While Elkanah was travelling around looking for a mission school site, Sarah was more or less convalescent at Fort Benton, where business went forward as usual. [179]

For all their original intentions, we have Agent Hatch's record that as early as August twentieth, the Mackeys were discussing the possibility of returning back down the river - after this briefest stay. Was Elkanah just going through the motions then, in order to have something respectable to report to the Foreign Board? Were he and his wife in fact disgusted with that barren country and aching to get back to civilization? The image of the weak-minded preacher and his frail, perhaps whining wife, springs easily to mind, especially since a few commentators suggest it in their reports. These commentators did not have as many facts as we, however, and having them, we find the caricature hard to support.

---

[178] ibid.

[179] It might interest some readers to know what business as usual looked like. The *Fort Benton Journal* gives an account of the business of this American Fur Company post, and has some nice literary flourishes thrown in, as well as commentary on various visitors, traders and Indians, rather in the style of 19th century journalism.

The rest of Elkanah's journal entry for 12 September gives some indication of the dilemma they felt they faced:

> [continued] And after mature, deliberate & prayerful consideration and consultation with Mr. Culbertson we have arrived at the conclusion that it is our duty to return. This conclusion has been reached not until after a violent struggle between our fee1ings of reluctance to leave our post, and the thought which kept constantly forcing itself upon our minds that it was our duty to do so under the circumstances.
>
> On Monday next we expect to start for the Mouth of the Judith River where the Mackinaw Boats will discharge the government freight intended for the Indians. Thence we will proceed with Mr. Culbertson in a Mackinaw boat to St. Lewis [sic].

In the "Private Letter" which Elkanah sent to Walter Lowrie along with his Report to the Foreign Board, we see more clearly the conflict in the minds of the Mackeys :

> . . .We are returning home on account of Mrs. Mackey's health. She was taken sick soon after we reached Fort Benton, confined to her bed one week & to her room two weeks. When she got able to walk out she still continued very weak & in a most distressing state of nervous derangement. In addition to this she was anticipating that epoch common to most married women & dreaded by all, even under the most favorable circumstances. In her weak & nervous state, as she could obtain no assistance medical or otherwise at Fort Benton, we concluded , after carefully & prayerfully considering the subject & consulting with Mr. Culbertson, that it was our duty to return. This conclusion cost us a violent struggle, but it seemed clearly to be our duty & we yield to the apparent indications of God's providence. There was no doubt in

> my mind that two lives were at stake in considering the question.[180]

The references to "two lives at stake" has an ominous ring, considered in retrospective.

Elkanah understood that their decision and actions might appear flighty to some:

> When you asked us last Spring to consider the question of Going to the Blackfeet & presented to our minds the reasons wh. led the Board to desire to establish a Mission among them at once, we felt that God in his providence was clearly calling us to that field. We felt that some risk would be incurred in going alone but hoped then another family would be obtained to accompany us. When we met you at Bellevue & found that no once else had been obtained to go, & while there also became aware of *her condition*, we still felt that it was our duty to go forward & trust the consequences to Him who had called us to the work.[181]

Sarah's pregnancy by itself, then, wasn't enough to turn them back, nor the fact that no other couple had been found to go with them, nor the combination of the two factors, which they were aware of before they went aboard the steamer to go up the Missouri. The reasons which did have sufficient weight in their minds to cause them to return had to do with Sarah's health, severe morning sickness combined at least at some points with other bouts of illness, and the apparent unavailability or inadequacy of medical help and mid-wifery at Fort Benton.

> She was sick a good deal & suffered very much during the trip across the country [Fort Union to Fort Benton], a great deal more than was known to any one except

---

[180] E. D. Mackey, "Private Letter," November 5, 1856

[181] ibid.

> ourselves and Him who sees all things. Still under the merciful care of a tender father, she was enabled to perform the whole long journey of four hundred miles by land & it was only after she was taken down & remained in that weak & nervous condition, that we were led to consider the question of returning.
>
> I consulted the physicians at Fort Pierre on our way down in regard to her health. He gave her some medicine which has helped her but she is still quite weak & nervous. [182]

Her diary reveals enough about Sarah Mackey to make this author confident in defending her character. Elkanah mentions her "nervous" condition and "nervous derangement," but she was no neurotic. It would be instructive to study what "nervous" meant in general usage in 1856. It sounds like the idea of returning was not even broached until she was confined to a sickbed at Fort Benton for a week. Agent Hatch heard of it six days after their arrival there. There may even have been other elements to her sickness beside pregnancy. The *Fort Benton Journal* continued to record a lot of illness among the Indians at or near the Fort during this period.

It is also interesting that the first physician Elkanah found was one at Fort Pierre, a mere thousand miles down the river from the place where she would otherwise have delivered her first child. (The baby was born the following January.) However, the Fort Benton *Journal* for July 15, a does mention a doctor, whom the Mackeys only missed by a month, "Dr. Lansdel started for across the Mountain with two wagons . . ."[183]

---

[182] ibid.

[183] M.H.S. Contributions, Vol X, Fort Benton Journal.

Dr. Richard H. Lansdel was the Indian Agent for the Flathead tribe from 1854, and became an important figure in Washington state. Just then he was headed back to Washington Territory, where a full-scale Indian war was boiling up in 1856, with Governor Isaac Stevens in the

The Culbertsons' imminent departure precipitated the Mackeys' decision, as Elkanah mentioned:

> . . .she was taken down & continued very weak and nervous up to the time of Mr. Culbertson's leaving the Fort to return on the 23rd of September. As she could obtain no medical aid there & Mr. & Mrs. Culbertson were about to leave us, we concluded, after prayerfully & deliberately considering the subject and consulting them that it was our duty to return.[184]

Elkanah certainly gave no indication of being discouraged or giving up. He concludes his Report with further references to seeing God's providence in their hardships:

> As the providence of God has sent us back I hope to be able to advance the interests of the Mission more by returning than we could have done by staying. There are several reasons why I hope to be able to do so, which need not here be mentioned, as we can talk them over when I see you. [185]

These things were written as he descended back down the river, but he does not sound like he is withdrawing in defeat.

The *Fort Benton Journal* for September 9 records: "This day Mr. Culbertson arrived from the boats left them at Cow Island, brought three Mules and four horses and four men."[186]

---

midst of it. It is doubtful Dr. Lansdale would have been available that winter. Curiously, his first wife was a Mary Culbertson of Troy, Ohio.

[184] E. D. Mackey, Report, November 13, 1856

[185] ibid.

[186] M.H. S. Contributions, Vol X, Fort Benton Journal

Jack Holterman mentions another significant event that took place at Fort Benton that summer.[187] Emissaries from the Bitterroot valley, west of the Continental Divide, included one who brought gold dust for trade. Alexander Culbertson was not sure whether to trust it or not, having no experience in gold assay:

> In the month of October a stranger appeared at the fort, coming by the trail from the southwest, now the Benton and Helena stage road; he was evidently an old mountaineer, and his object was to purchase supplies. Producing a sack, he displayed a quantity of yellow dust which he claimed was gold, and for which he demanded' $1 000.00, offering to take it all in goods.
>
> Nothing was known at the fort of the existence of gold in the adjoining country and Major Culbertson was loth to accept the proffered dust, having doubts of its genuineness. Besides, even if it was gold, he was uncertain of its value . . ., when an employee of the fort, a young man named Ray [Wray?] [by giving] assurances as to the genuineness of the gold and the value of the quantity offered, induced Major Culbertson to accept it.
>
> Still doubtful, however, he made it a private transaction, charging goods to his own account. The mountaineer was very reticent as to the locality where he obtained the gold, but in answer to numerous questions, he stated that he had been engaged in prospecting for a considerable period in the mountains to the southwest, that his wanderings had been made alone, and that he had found plenty of gold. Receiving in exchange for his gold dust a supply of horses, arms, ammunition, blankets, tobacco, provisions and other supplies, he quietly left the fort on his return to the mountains.
>
> Major Culbertson never saw or heard of him again, and was ignorant even of his name. The following

---

[187] Holterman, *King of the High Missouri*, pp125-6

> year he sent the gold through the hands of Mr. Chouteau to the mint and in due time received as the yield thereof $1,525.00, the dust having proved remarkably pure gold."[188]

It was later said this was the first gold to come through Benton from what became the Montana Gold Rush. [189]

Agent Hatch records their departure from Fort Benton September 15th, in his usual laconic style, "Mr. Culbertson and wife, missionary and wife started by land down the river."[190] The Fort Benton Journal records:

> . . .This day A. Culbertson started for the Judith with Two wagons and his bugey. The minister and his Wife left with him. Major Hatch left in the small boat with One Man to meet the boats, have left in the Fort three Men and two families .[191]

The *Fort Benton Journal* contains interesting details about the construction of a Mackinaw on the upper river

---

188 *M. H. S. Contributions, Vol X,* Notes and References to "Fort Benton Journal", p 246-47, citing *Leeson's History of Montana,* 1885, page 210. which in turn is quoting Lieut. Bradley in a letter, Sept. 21, 1875, to the *Helena Herald* in which he told the story as he heard it from Culbertson who gave the year as 1856.

189 It is estimated that Last Chance Gulch (in what is now Helena, the capital of Montana) produced 19 million dollars worth of gold – at 1860's valuation, about 1/60th of today's value. Another source estimates the Grasshopper Creek region alone produced another 184 million dollars worth of gold at today's prices. Using that yardstick, totals from the Montana gold rush run into many billions.

190 M. H. S. Contributions, vol X. Agent Hatch's Diary. NOTE that Hatch's date for the Culbertson and Mackey departure (as indicated by his journal date) is a week earlier than the one Elkanah gives for "Mr. Culbertson". Elkanah must have dated his" departure" from the time they left the Judith.

191 M. H. S. Contributions, vol X, Fort Benton *Journal*

before the Mackeys arrived. This may have been the craft upon which the Mackeys were about to travel down to Ft. Union, although another record shows a Mackinaw being built at Fort Union that summer.

Mackinaws were primarily downstream boats, unlike the sturdier keelboats which were cordelled upriver. Although similar in appearance to a small, cabinless keelboat, they were constructed with flat bottoms and were therefore better suited to shallower water, while still being able to carry ample cargo. A Mackinaw only required a crew of five or six, while a keelboat required a fur company "brigade" of 20 to 40 men. A Mackinaw could go about a hundred miles a day downstream, against a keelboat's 15 miles upstream.

Earlier the Journal indicates there was a plan in place to build another boat in addition to the ones that had been brought up the river that year:

> *Mon. 14 April* --. . .Commenced on the only Boat we intend to build this year 85 ft by 12 3/4 Hauled up to Fort our last years Boat but the wind blew too strong for us to bring up the large Keel - Had her cleaned, however . . .
>
> *Tues 15* . . .Had our big Keel at long last brought up to Fort. This is her first visit to these upper regions and we hope it will be her only one, as she is by far too big for our river - Very windy as usual Crossed our logs and had them hauled into Fort.. . .
>
> *Sat. 26* - . . . Planked up sides of our new Boat . . .
>
> *Wed 30* – Finished our New Boat, the biggest ever made here, and raised her up for caulking . . .
>
> *Fri. 2 May* . . . Finished Caulking our new Boat and launched her.

Only seventeen days from first mention, the boat was finished! Apparently the wood had already been hauled and possibly even sawed up beforehand – because, as we see, the whole process took about a month on the next boat they built.

The next day we see a curious feature of their nautical preparations:

> *Sat 3.* -- . . .Caulked our Big Keel Boat and sunk her. Also had our old Boat hauled out and put on the Stocks to dry.

Since they sunk the "old boat" three days later, and then bailed them both out two days after, this appears to have been a regular part of the spring ritual - apparently thus swelling the lumber of the hulls to make them tight.

On the 12th of May the three loaded boats set out "for the Yellowstone," that is for Fort Union with the winter's take of robes traded from the Indians.

Three months later additional instructions arrived at Fort Benton, and work commenced on another Mackinaw. The Journal gives a wonderful degree of detail about it's construction:

> *22 July* - This evening an express arrived from the boats at the point Frenchman [192] requiring a boat sixty feet long.
>
> *23 July* - . . .Put up three wagons to get timber from the mountain getting things in preparation for sawing the boat timber.
>
> *24 July* - This day started three wagons to the Mountains and four Men for boat timber, four men at work on the saws. . .
>
> *25 July* - Four men on the saws turned off fourteen planks put up two more logs on the pit - Three men at work on boat nails …

---

[192] Frenchman's Point was the site of an old post run by Antoine Janis for Rocky Mt. Fur Co. 50 miles above Fort Union and the Yellowstone.

These instructions were received at Fort Benton four days before Culbertsons and Mackeys set out overland from Ft. Union.

26 July – Four men at work on the saws. …three men making nails, the fort full of Indians. . .

28 July – The Men at work on the saws. Sent a wagon after Wood. . .

29 July -- . . .This day Shouquet [Chouquette] … Smith . . . Indian with Six mules and a horse started to Meet Mr. Culbertson on Milk River with letters for Mr. Dawson and Mr. C.

30 July -- . . .This day finished sawing the bottom of the boat . . .

31 July -- . . . the Carpenters started for the Teton with two men and one wagon to cut nees [knees] and other timber for the boat. Two of my wagons arrived from the Mountain with elleven logs and all the men and cattle. One wagon brock down at the dry fork [193] with seven logs.

1 Aug – Sent the Men after the brocken wagon and timber. They arrived this afternoon and brought the wagons into the Fort. Crossed all the oxen. The Fort full of Indians again.

2 Aug – This day rafted and hauled the timber into the Fort Sent two Waggons on the Teton for the Carpenter returned brought all the nees [knees] and other timber for the boat . . .

Mon 4 Aug -- . . .This day the Carpenters and two Men at work dressing plank for the boat four men at Work on the Saws. Sent two Men on the Teton with a wagon for timber to lay the bottom of the boat on . . .

5 Aug – All hands at work on the boat dressed the bottom plank and sawed the bars.

6 Aug – Commenced laying the bottom of the Boat and spliting the knees, finished laying the bottom of the boat commenced sawing the sides.

7 Aug --This day turned the bottom of the boat, four men sawing the sides

8 Aug – All hands at work on the boat.

---

[193] Dry Fork may be Spring Coulee, which is joined by Nine Mile Coulee on the route to the Shonkin end of the Highwood Mts.

9 Aug – Planking the sides of the boat Six men on the Saws.

11 Aug – This day finished sawing the sides of the boat.

12 Aug --The boat planked up Whitewashing the Fort finished the boat with the exception of the caulking

13 Aug – The Boat nearly finished for launching.

14 Aug – This day the boat started to meet Mr. Dawson with five men and F. Wray in Charge. Major Hatch arrived. . .

And the next day, as we've seen, the Mackeys and Culbertsons ended their overland wagon trip and reached their long-anticipated destination, at Fort Benton.

Mackinaw on the Missouri from an 1833 aquatint by Outhwaite based on a Karl Bodmer watercolor

CHAPTER FIVE - Two Lives At Stake

Elkanah and Sarah's return trip for the conscious purpose of saving two lives began with a short side-trip down the Missouri from Fort Benton to the mouth of the Judith river, as he wrote in his journal:

> *Thursday, September 18th.* On Monday the 15th we left Fort Benton & reached our camp above the mouth of the Judith this afternoon. Mrs. M. is very weak and nervous but has stood the trip of four days over the Prairies in a carriage better than we expected. A large number of Flatheads, Pend O'Reilles [Pen d'Oreilles] & Paeguns accompanied us from the Fort and joined the other Indians here encamped. The whole of the Gros Ventres and part of the Paeguns were here when we came. The boats will not reach here for two or three days.
>
> *Friday, September 19th.* This evening I had a conference in Mr. Culbertson's tent with Lame Bull and Spotted Cow, the 1st and 2nd chief of the Paegun band of Blackfoot Indians. I explained to them my object in coming to the country; told them that I was now going down to tell those who had sent us there what I had seen & heard & I wanted to know before going if they were willing that we white men & women should come & live among them with the object in view wh. I had described & whether they wld. be kind & friendly to them & protect them.
>
> They said that so far as they were concerned they were perfectly willing and would be their friends and protectors but they wanted to consult the other chiefs before giving me a final answer.

Elkanah's Report tells how he took advantage of the gathering of Indians for the 1856 annuity distribution at the Judith River, to try to fulfill a few points of his commission from the Foreign Board. There he spoke with some of the most important chiefs:

> When we reached the mouth of the Judith we found the Paeguns encamped on the South side of the Missouri & the Gros Ventres on the North, the same side upon which we pitched our tents. On the 19th of Sept. two of the principal chiefs, Lame Bull and Spotted Cow, came across the river to our camp. I embraced this opportunity of holding a council with them, explaining to them somewhat in detail the objects of our Mission, stating at the same time that we were about to return down the river with Mr. Culbertson to those who had sent us to tell them what we had seen & what we had heard, and we wished to know whether they were willing that white men & women should come & live in their country having in view the objects I had stated. Lame Bull replied that so far as they were concerned they would be entirely willing, but that in a matter of as much importance, he would prefer to bring the subject up before all the chiefs of his band before giving me a final answer and that he would give me an answer before we started down the river. The next day he came over again to our camp & made reply in substance as follows.
>
> "I have brought the matter before all the chiefs in council. Their judgment agrees with mine. We would be very glad to have white men & women come & live among us to carry out the objects you have stated, and if they come up the river when the boat returns again, we will be their friends and listen to their words. We are satisfied that white men are *our* friends, if they were not they would not go to the trouble of sending us so many valuable presents every year. We desire them to come &

teach us about the Great Spirit & tell us plenty of good things.[194]

Ne-Tannay, The Only Chief, or Stam-yehk-sas-ci-cay, Lame Bull, Piegan Chief, by Gustavus Sohon, 1855.

"When we catch a wild animal on the prairie & attempt to tame him we sometimes find it very hard. It may take a long time & a great deal of patience. but almost any animal can be tamed by kindness & perseverance. We have been running wild on the prairie and now we want the white sons & daughters of our Great Father to come to our country & tame us.

"We have been like crying children. When a child is bad & cries and you tell it *mowpeet,* i.e. be quiet, and teach it to be good, then it stops crying. *We* want to

---

[194] Jack Holterman in his monograph "Little Dog," p. 8, (typescript sent by Holterman to author) says Little Dog, who became head chief of the Piegans with the death of Lame Bull in 1857, talked to a Jesuit at St. Ignatius Mission and "confided to the priest that the whites east of the mountains neglected to discuss religion with the Indians."

> *mowpeet,*[195] and be like good children. We wish you to tell those good people who sent you here what you have seen & heard. We have a fine country & we are not ashamed to have white men come & see it. If we have anything that you wish to carry home with you to show your people, mention it & we will freely give it to you. This is our answer to what you have said to us."

Elkanah's Journal entries don't give the same detail as his Report about the rhetoric used on this occasion, but they contain some additional data:

> *Sat. Sept. 20th.* Lame Bull came to-day to Mr. Culbertson's tent. I had another conference with him in regard to our mission. He said he had consulted all the other chiefs & that they were all of the same opinion as himself. He made quite a speech to me.
>
> The similes he used were that of the wild animal caught on the prairie and a bad, ungovernable child. I am to have a conference tomorrow morning with the chiefs of the Gros Ventres.
>
> *Sabbath, Sept. 21st.* Went down to-day with Mr. Monroe to the camp of the Gros Ventres, about two miles below our camp on the bank of the river. All the chiefs assembled in the tent of the principal one. They are five in number, viz.
>
> 1. The Bear Shirt, or Bearded Chief
> 2. The Eagle Boss Rib
> 3. The Star Robe
> 4. The Sitting Squaw &
> 5. The Two Elks.
>
> I made to them explanations similar to those I had made to the Paegun chiefs & each one replied separately

---

195 Holterman, pp 126-7, transliterates this as *maupit* and says it is properly *amaupit* "shut-up"

> that they would be very glad to have white men & women to come to live among them to teach them. During my conference with them the Mackinaw boats came up & stopped in front of the camp.
>
> We moved our tents down about noon & pitched them in front of the Grosventres, & to-day has been one of bustle and business unloading the boats. Oh! that men who do business among the Indians would honor the Sabbath & thus teach them one of the lessons of Christianity.

Elkanah's Report summarizes:

> On the 21st of Sept. I went to the camp of the Gros Ventres accompanied by my interpreter. The chiefs were all assembled in the lodge of the principal chief, *Bear Shirt*. I explained to them as I had done to the Paeguns the objects of our Mission, & asked them if they would be friends of the white men & women who would come to their country with such objects in view. They each replied separately in substance the same, that they would be very glad to have them come & would be their friends.
>
> The other two bands, the Bloods and Blackfeet, for some cause unknown to us, did not reach the Judith & I was obliged to leave without seeing them. But there is no doubt that if I had seen them the result would have been the same, as it was in relation to the other two bands. [196]

Agent Hatch, who had written September 12, "This prairie is literally covered with lodges," completed the distribution of the annuities at the Mouth of the Judith :

> *September 22*: Beautiful morning, Received the goods and distributed nearly all of them – shall finish in the

[196] E. D. Mackey, Report, November 13, 1856

morning - everything went off quickly - about 8,000 Indians present. One small row. [197]

Elkanah witnessed what may have been the largest gathering of Native Americans to take place in the region. He wrote:

> *Tues. Sept. 23.* Yesterday and to-day the goods were delivered to the Indians by Major Hatch, the Government agent. I spoke to Little Dog, one of the Paegun Chiefs, in regard to our Mission. He said Lame Bull told him & the other chiefs what I had said & that they were all very much pleased & would he glad to have missionaries come and tell then plenty of good things. We left the mouth of the Judith about noon and this evening below the Rapids on our way down the River. Our company consists of Mr. Culbertson & his family, Major Hatch, Mr. Bennett, Mr. John Culbertson and about thirty five men to row and cook.

The Culbertsons and Mackeys continued down the river after the annuities distribution - probably via the three keelboats[198] which had brought the annuities up.

They descended the river to Fort Union. Jack Holterman speculates it was at this juncture that they encountered the infamous Sir St. George Gore, "The Irish Nimrod." As Holterman says "rarely has a man been so properly named."[199] But it seems unlikely his calendar is right about this. We know Jim Bridger joined the topographers in July at Fort Union, and we think Gore was with him then.

Elkanah's Journal entry for their arrival back at Fort Union:

---

[197] "Any Give-away Draws", Joel F. Overholser, *River Press* article, no doubt Hatch's Diary entry from M. H. .S Contributions, Vol X.
[198] ibid.
[199] Holterman, *King of the High Missouri*, p. 127

Thursday, Oct. 2nd. Reached Fort Union to-day in nine days from the Judith. Killed and butchered three Buffalos on our way down a& shot several Grizzly Bears, three of which would no doubt die but they ran off too far for us to get them. Were not obliged to stop at all on account of the wind wh. was something unusual.

Major Hatch leaves us here to go across by land by way of Pembina and St. Paul. Col. Vaughan and his Squaw go with us down as far as Fort Pierre. The boat of Pecott [Picotte] & Co. we learn brought up the Small Pox or something, like of wh. nine children have died at Fort William and we learn that the Indians below have also taken the same disease.

From Fort Union, the travelers continued down the river, probably in the same Mackinaw boat.

Sab. Oct. 6th. [NOTE he mixed up the date here.] Killed three bufalos, the last we saw.

Wed. Oct. 8th. Reached Fort Berthold this morning being detained by wind only about an hour just after leaving Fort Union on Fri. at noon. There has been only one or two cases here of the above mentioned disease. Detained about two hours & then proceeded on towards Fort Clarke.

Friday, October 10th. Reached Fort Clarke yesterday afternoon. Col. Vaughan had a conference with the Arickerees yesterday & delivered them some presents this morning. They have had sixty deaths among them from that disease. We left the Fort this morning about ten o'clk. The Mandans, whom we saw up the river a day or two ago were to have been here to receive a present but did not come before we left. Their present will be delivered to them when they come.

Monday, October 13th. Reached Little Soldier's village of dirt lodges. He has some 12 or 15 lodges. They are a small band of the Yancktonie Sioux -- who have separated from the rest & are trying to cultivate the soil to obtain part of their subsistence. Game in their country is becoming scarce.

Thursday, October 16th. We got under way this morning again soon after sun up. We were stopped on Tuesday about ten o'clk. by the wind & lay all day Tuesday & yesterday at Rush Point, the wind blowing a gale & the river rolling like a miniature sea. Rush Point is the second above the Moreau.

Met a small party of Yancktones this morning and gave them some sugar, coffee & tobacco and got from them some venison.

Monday, October 20th. Left Fort Pierre this morning, having reached there Sat. about three o'clk. Consulted Dr. Crowell about Mrs. Mackey's health. He came down to see her & sent her some medicine. He is a very kind, pleasant, gentlemanly man. He also sent her down a bottle of Plumb Jelly. Mr. Atkinson also came to see her & sent her a box of nice little nic—nacs. Mrs. A. was not well & could not come down.

God has every where raised up for us kind & sympathizing friends, for wh. we bless his name. We got a large pack of letters from friends, but no papers or letters from New York. We were very much disappointed in this. Mrs. Culbertson gave me a buffalo robe this morning, a fine one [200] & Mrs. M. some pickles and other nic nacs --

Wed. Oct. 22nd. Reached Fort Lookout last evening & left this morning about nine or ten o'clock.

---

[200] Wilmer Mackey Sanner notes that Mrs. Mackey gave this robe to her daughter, Laura, who made good use of it for her family for a period of 40 years -- until it was worn out.

Dr. [McCruder/McGruder] sent Mrs. Mackey down a fine piece of fresh beef. 30 or 40 lbs.

Sat. Oct. 25th. Reached Fort Randall this morning, soon after breakfast & were detained 3 or 4 hours. The Quarter Master there hired eight of our men for the Winter. Three soldiers discharged there for inability, got on our boat to go down to St. Louis. A great many of the Soldiers there have deserted. Two deserters on the shore hailed us this evening & one of them got aboard to deliver himself up to the Lieutenant below. The other went on up towards the Fort. They had lost all their provisions & rifles in attempting to cross L'eau qui court, on a raft.

Monday, Oct. 27th. Yesterday our deserter was among the missing. We were obliged by the wind to lay up about half the day.

To-day we made a fine run, passed the River a' Jaques about three o'clk. a strong stern wind blowing --

Tuesday, Oct. 28th. Made a fine run to-day.

Wed. Oct. 29th. Ran but a few miles & were obliged to lay up the rest of the day on account of the wind.

Thurs. Oct. 30th. Ran a few miles this morning and were stopped by the wind. Mr. C. took the yawl with 5 or 6 men & went on to Bruyer's to get provisions. He lives on the Big Sioux, two or three miles above its mouth. Our provisions are getting quite short. Mr. Paul shot us a wild turkey yesterday and a prairie hen today.

Soon after Mr. C. started we moved on down some eight or ten miles farther and were stopped again by the wind just above a snaggy bend. Moved down a few miles farther in the evening.

Fri. Oct. 31st. Reached the mouth of the Big Sioux this morning soon after breakfast. Mr. C. & his party soon came down from Bruyer's with provisions. Stopped at Sioux City where we detained 3 or four hours. Nearly all the men got drunk. It is a blessing that we have a sober pilot. Tom West, one of the discharged soldiers, was very bad & threw himself overboard to drown himself. The boat was stopped & he was rescued from a watery grave. The men have been in bad order for pulling. Too much steam on.

Sat. Nov. 1st. Men all sober, made a good run.

Mon. Nov. 3rd. Made a good run yesterday. I spoke to the men urging them to seek an interest in [Christ/life]. May the Holy Spirit water the seed sown in faith. To-day ran very well, but got on a snag wh. detained [us] near an hour. The men had to get out in the cold water. There was but a plank between us & death & that plank was across a snag ready to be broken. Passed Florence, Omaha, & c.

Tues. Nov. 4th. Stopped at Bellevue & got three boxes that were left in the Spring. Old Mrs. Allen is very low, will probably not recover. Mrs. Schemousky has been very low but is now better. Stopped at St. Mary & got some apples, provisions, & c., and camped some 30 miles below.

Wed. Nov. 5. Started early, a fine morning, ran till ten o'clk. & were laid up by the wind a few miles below Nebraska City. The wind lulled a little towards evening, we dropped a few miles farther down and found a better camp.

Still in the Mackinaw boat, Elkanah wrote his "Private Letter," headed "On the Missouri River Above St. Joseph Nov 5-/56," and beginning:

My Dear Sir, A Mackinaw Boat is not a very good place for writing letters, but as I may not be able to write you all I wish to after we get on a Steamboat I commence a letter now.[201]

At normal rates of travel, by mackinaw from Fort Union to St. Louis would take about 22 days.

Thurs. Nov. 6. Laid up all day by the wind. About nine o'clock at night three men & a lady came to the boat to get something eat. They had been overtaken by the night not far from our camp.

Fri. Nov. 7. Laid by all day on account of wind. About an inch of snow fell last night. It has been snowing a little to-day at intervals & this evening is still cloudy, but not blowing so much. Mr. Bennett took passage in a wagon bound for St. Joseph yesterday. Mr. Vascas [Vasquez] and John Culbertson started for St. Jo. by land, with the mules. To-day we have had a wild turkey, plenty of fresh apples, & c. -- faring sumptuously every day on the fat of the land.

Sat. Nov. 8. A beautiful calm morning, but the river is full of floating ice. Our boat cannot run. About ten o'clk. Mr. Culbertson & his family and Mrs. Mackey & I took passage in two wagons that came by, bound for St. Joe, leaving Mr. Paul in charge of the boat & men and the principal part of our baggage. We had a hundred miles to go by land to St. Jo. Mrs. Mackey seems to have been providentially strengthened for the emergency.

Tues. Nov. 11. Reached St. Jo. to-day, about one o' clk. Mrs. Mackey is very tired but has stood the trip better than we expected. There has not been a time since we left Fort Benton when she could have stood a trip without very great inconvenience.

---

[201] E. D. Mackey, Private Letter, November 5, 1856

Report 160
40

St. Joseph Mo.
Nov. 13 - 1856

My Dear Sir,

We reached this point two days ago and are now waiting for a Steamboat which is daily expected up from St. Louis. I will embrace this opportunity of giving you an sketch of what we have done since leaving Fort Union on the 26th of July.

Our journey from there to Fort Benton occupied us just three weeks. During this time we were dwellers in tents & never set foot in human habitation. Our way led us up the Missouri to the mouth of Milk River thence up Milk River until we passed the Bear's Paw mountains, & then across a wide

Beginning of Elkanah's Report to the Missions Board

> *Wed. Nov. 12.* Called to-day on Rev. Mr. Schenck the Pres. Minister in St. Jo. Found him a very pleasant man.

> *Thurs. Nov. 13.* Mr. Schenck called to-day and this evening I went to their prayer meeting. Enjoyed it very much & made several pleasant acquaintances. Gave them a little talk about the Blackfoot Mission.

The Mackeys spent several days there, giving Elkanah time to compose his Report, headed, "St. Joseph, Mo- Nov 13 - 1856," and which begins, "My Dear Sir, We reached this point two days ago and are now waiting for a Steamboat which is daily expected up from St. Louis." A few days later they went aboard the same steamboat which had brought them up the river, the *St. Mary*..

> *Fri. Nov. 14.* The Boat *St. Mary* reached here from St. Louis last night. We are now on board of her & started about sundown for St. Louis. Our baggage has not come yet. Paul, we learn left the boat on Tues. & is bringing on the freight in wagons. They cannot be far from here now. We expect our freight to come down on the next boat.

> *Wed. Nov. 19th.* Reached St. Louis this evening & took lodgings at the Virginia Hotel to await the coming of our baggage.

Nearing St. Louis, Elkanah appended a postscript to his Report:

> Nov 19th On the Steamboat *St. Mary*
>
> We expect to reach St. Louis to-day & home some time next week. After I get Mrs. Mackey comfortably located for the Winter I will go on to New York. In the mean time let me hear from you at New London, Pa. Is there any particular time at which you would wish me

to be in New York? – Since we came to Fort Pierre, Mrs. Mackey's health with some fluctuations has been gradually improving, & she is now much stronger than when we left Ft. Benton.

Very truly & affectionately yours & c. E. D. Mackey

Walter Lowrie, Esq.
23 Centre St.
New York, --

Several sections of Elkanah's Report pertaining to the specifics of the proposed Mission School, etcetera, have been quoted already. Parts of the preamble discussing the Mackey's unexpected return have also been cited. That introductory segment concludes:

> There is one thing of which you may be fully assured – that it could not possibly have been any deleterious influences of climate that caused Mrs. Mackey's sickness. The climate is without doubt one of the most healthy in the world. The situation & character of the country itself might testify to this; and this testimony is confirmed by the experience of those who have resided in the country as well as by my own individual experience. My health during our sojourn there was uninterrupted. * [this asterisk was placed here in the original handwritten document, but since no footnote follows, it may have indicated emphasis.]
>
> I will now proceed to take up in order the points mentioned in our instructions upon which you desire information.[202]

The first section of the body of the Report is entitled "I. The Manner of Our Reception," yet it says little about the Mackey's relations with any Blackfoot during their trip

---

[202] ibid

to and stay at Fort Benton. The exceptions are the various mentions of Mrs. Culbertson and one reference to seeing "Gros Ventres and Paegun" hunters who "greeted us with a hearty welcome" during the overland trip from Fort Union. The journey was far too brief for the forming of real relationships. However "The Manner of Our Reception" has a generally positive note:

> It has been already mentioned in passing that we were kindly received & greeted with a hearty welcome. We had many opportunities of hearing expressions of kind feeling toward us, both on our way to the Fort from Indians whom we met & also from those whom we saw after we reached there. The different bands of the nation were all assembled at the mouth of the Judith River about four weeks after we reached the Fort, for the purpose of receiving their annuities.
>
> This was judged to be the time at which I could best see the chiefs & hold with them a formal council. I accordingly remained at the Fort holding divine service in English once every Sabbath in Mr. Culbertson's Room, and giving religious instruction to the Indians about, as opportunity from time to time offered, explaining to them in familiar language the principles & precepts of the Christian religion & the objects we had in view in coming to their country.

The Report continues with the sections given above, in which Elkanah describes his meetings with the two chiefs at the Judith River. After that he continues with the paragraphs quoted earlier concerning the Mission Boarding School, which concludes:

> Our impressions of the Blackfoot character compared with that of other Indians have been very favorable. On this point we are not so well qualified to speak with reference to the males of the nation as we would have been after a longer acquaintance. But with

reference to Mrs. Culbertson we can speak more particularly, as we have been in close contact with her ever since we met her at Fort Pierre on our way up the River & have had an opportunity of seeing her under a variety of circumstances.

If her character may be taken as an index to the character of the nation, our impressions are of the most favorable kind. She has at all times been to us a fine & firm friend & has fully redeemed the promise she voluntarily made when we first met her that she would be Mrs. Mackey's friend when we got to the country of the Blackfeet. She has a noble, kind & generous heart, quick to detect the wants of those around her & prompt to relieve them. We have contracted for her a strong & we trust a lasting personal friendship, and attachment –

I cannot forebear mentioning also the kindnesses which under all circumstances Mr. Culbertson has shown us & especially the kindness & sympathy he has ever manifested towards Mrs. Mackey under the trying circumstances in which she has been placed. May God reward him for his constant and unvarying kindness towards us!

For our freight which was to have been ten cents a pound to Fort Benton, he charged but nine thus lessening our expense by about thirty two dollars in that particular item, [Thus we may calculate they took about 3200 pounds of freight!] and when we determined to return home he offered to store our goods free of charge until next Spring.

Again, from the time the Steam Boat left us at Fort Union in July until we left the Mackinaw Boat a few days ago, we have been at his expense for board & transportation. This would be a considerable item, particularly if estimated at the rates prevailing in that upper country: For all this he charges us nothing -- [203]

[203] ibid

I cannot forbear mentioning here also the kindness which under all circumstances Mr. Culbertson has shown us & especially the kindness & sympathy he has ever manifested towards Mrs. Mackey under the trying circumstances in which she has been placed. May God reward him for his constant & unvarying kindness towards us!

Praises for Mr. Culbertson in Elkanah's Report

In the final passages of his Report, Elkanah speaks with apparent confidence in his intention of continuing the Blackfoot Mission:

> I have given you above briefly as I could the results of our mission thus far. I would have dwelt more in detail upon some points but I expect in a short time to see you & then we can talk them over more at length.
>
> What I now propose to the Board is this. To obtain a reinforcement of missionaries & return next Spring to occupy the field which has thus been opened. Mrs. Mackey will probably not be able to return with me, but if she is well enough to remain with her friends, though it will be a trial for us to separate, yet we will willingly endure that trial, provided I am allowed to return again in the Fall. I have become acquainted with the Indians, the localities of the country, the state of things existing there & c., and the knowledge I have

> gained on these and other points could at once be made available.
>
> On this we can consult more fully when I see you.[204]

At the time he wrote his report, the next stop on the Mackeys' return trip was to be St. Louis. Elkanah had certainly not stopped thinking ahead. We know from his "Private Letter" that he was expecting a propaganda battle, and already planning his tactics, "I fear the Catholics in St. Louis will take advantage of our return. I intend calling on Dr. Rice when we reach there to consult him about publishing the state of the case."[205]

> *Thurs. Nov. 20th.* How little we know what is best for us. If we had got our baggage on the same boat with ourselves it would all have been burnt up last night in the warehouse of Theobald & Co. Heard Dr. Anderson preach.

> *Sat. Nov. 22.* Our baggage came last night in the *Admiral*. I have repacked such as needed repacking & will have it sent off on Monday morning.

> *Sabbath, Nov. 23.* Heard Dr. [N. L./A. L.] Rice preach today. Text: "The kingdom of God is not meat & drink but righteousness &peace & joy in the Holy Ghost."

From St. Louis, Elkanah and Sarah traveled east by rail, passing through Indiana, West Virginia, to Maryland, where they stayed with Elkanah's sister, Jane Mackey Kelso:

---

[204] ibid.

[205] E. D. Mackey, "Private Letter," November 5, 1856

Mon. Nov. 24. Left St. Louis for home this morning. Reached Indianapolis about ten at night & stopped until morning. Sarah became very sick & threw up in the cars before we came to our stopping place.

Tues. Nov. 25. Stopped for the night at Wheeling. Met a poor old lady in the cars who had been taken sick far from home & was out of money. Gave her a dollar to pay for her lodgings & paid for her supper.

Wed. Nov. 26. Stopped for the night at Cumberland.

Thurs. Nov. 27. Reached Balt. about dark, intending to remain with Jane [Elkanah's sister, Jane (Mackey) Kelso] until Sat.

The final entry of the Diary/Journal is dated *Sat. Nov. 29* : "Reached Spring Run [206] about one o'clk., having been absent 7 months & one day."

The concluding words of Elkanah's Blackfoot Mission journal are three scripture verses:

Go ye into all the world and preach the gospel to every creature. **Mark 16:15**

Let your loins be girded about, and your lights burning. **Luke 12:35**

---

206 Elkanah's father, William, is the earliest proven ancestor. But "Spring Run" may be a key. Robert Mackey, tanner, b. ca. 1720, had a son, David b. ca. 1745, who received "Spring Run" land from Robert in 1767 and 1771; he m. Martha, had four sons and a dau. mentioned in David's will, 1788. It's likely that one of them: Robert, John, David, or William, had a son William, who married Sarah Martin, who in turn had Elkanah, b. 1826, who brought his pregnant wife, Sarah, home from Montana to "Spring Run" in 1856. Not definite but notable. (Most of the land record data from Beatrice Doughtie's *Mackey Family*.)

***And lo I am with you always even unto the end of the world.* Matthew 28:20**

When or and whether he met with the Foreign Missions Board we have not been able to find. In fact, the last mention of his name in connection with the Blackfoot mission, seems to be this from the General Assembly of the Presbyterian church the next year:

> Rev. Elkanah D. Mackey, of the presbytery of Newcastle, and Mrs. Mackey, were appointed to commence this mission , and left home in the month of June, for that purpose, but did not reach Fort Benton, the proposed headquarters of the mission, until the middle of August. From Fort Union they had to travel by wagons, using tents at night, to Fort Benton, and were three weeks in performing this journey. They were cordially received by the Indians, and much gratification was expressed at the prospect of having Christian missionaries to live among them. Mrs. Mackey's health failed, however; and Mr. Mackey felt it his duty to return with her after a sojourn of six weeks at Fort Benton, hoping to be able to return in the spring and resume his work.
>
> Mr. Mackey has communicated much valuable information about the Indian tribes in that region, their character and habits, the nature of the climate, the soil, and productions of the country, and on various other topics; all of which go to show the great importance of sustaining a permanent mission among that people. As they are migratory in their habits, however, and dwell almost altogether in tents, very little good can be effected for them except by establishing a boarding school for their children. [207]

[207] GA PCUSA 1857 Minutes and Reports

What considerations were guiding the Foreign Board as it considered its strategy for the Blackfoot Mission? The same report goes on:

> This cannot be done, however, without large expense; and as it is presumed the Government would cheerfully [!] make an appropriation for this purpose. a proposition to this effect has been submitted to them; until this has been acted upon, no further measures will be adopted for carrying on the mission. [208]

This seems a rather abrupt ending to the whole enterprise! It would be sad to think that the decisions were made solely on the basis of money. In the correspondence of Lowrie and Elkanah the various financial scenarios had been discussed. Government money was not spoken of as a *sine qua non*, but rather as the difference between a big school and a small one.

So, without having any written confirmation beyond what has already been copied here, it seems likely the Mackeys had been found wanting. Although we have further correspondence between various parties, including Alexander Culbertson and Walter Lowrie, no other mention of the Mackeys is extant. One might imagine communication, perhaps indirect ones through their various connections by which Lowrie asks Culbertson to assess the Mackeys and Culbertson reports that in his opinion they are too soft for the job. But that is purely speculative.

Nevertheless the stated reason for the hold-up, and thus presumably the failure to re-staff and re-commission the Blackfoot Mission, was the failure of federal funds to appear. Early the following spring Lowrie sent this proposition to Washington:

---

[208] ibid.

Mission House
New York, Feb 16, 1857

Geo W. Manypenny Esqu
Commissioner of Indian Affairs
Sir

The Board of Foreign Missions of the Presbyterian Church, beg leave to submit to the Department, two proposals for Missionary, Educational, and agricultural operations among the Blackfeet Indians. Should either of these proposals meet the approbation of the Department, the Board will take measures at once to carry it into operation.

1. The First proposal contemplates a school of thirty or forty children of both sexes, to be boarded, clothed and taught, by the mission, as in other boarding schools.

For school buildings it is estimated that $8,500 will be required, and for commencing the farm $1500; for both $10,000. Of this sum the Department to furnish 7,500 and the Board from their own funds ¼ more, 2,500 . . .

To sustain the school and farm, it is estimated that $6,500 will be required annually, the number of scholars for the first year being estimated at thirty, and for succeeding years at forty

Of this sum the Department to furnish ¾ 4,875, And the Board ¼ 1,625 . . .

The Department also to furnish on the ground:

1 good yoke of oxen
1 ox cart
1 light one horse cart % harness
1 plow, 1 set harrow teeth & two log chains

We have no objection that a stipulation be inserted in the contract to this effect – That an exact account be kept of all expenses for the buildings and farm, including the traveling expenses of the missionaries in reaching the station, and their salaries & support, and if less than $10,000 be required, the

Department to pay only ¾ of the sum actually expended. The same provision also in regard to the school if less than $6,500 be required for its support.

2. The other proposal contemplates the commencement of these efforts on a smaller scale, leaving it to future arrangements, between the Department and the Board, to enlarge the school, and of course the buildings and the farm, if favorable circumstances, and the feelings of the Indians, should make that desirable.

This proposal contemplates a school of 12 or 15 children only … for the school buildings it is estimated … $5000 … To sustain the school & farm annually it is estimated … $3,500 …

It will be seen that in both proposals, a farm is deemed indispensable, both for the benefit of the school, and the best interests of the Indians. No permanent benefit will result from any agency for the good of the people, unless they are taught the absolute necessity of supporting themselves, by cultivation of the soil. The mission farm will bring that fully before them, and at an expense to the Department of less than ¼ of what it will cost to have a government farm. If the farm succeeds, the expense of the school will be greatly reduced, and... will secure the enlargement of the school to the full extent of the means furnished.

I am Sir Respectfully
your obt Svt
Walter Lowrie
Sec't'y [209]

Apparently, as seems inevitable with applications to governing bodies, this proposal hung fire for a time. It says something about the day and age that Lowrie seems to have sent a follow-up letter asking for a decision within

---

[209] Walter Lowrie, LTR, to Geo. W. Manypenny, Feb 16 1857, (also in Klett, "Missionary Endeavors")

three weeks! The reply which the "Department" then sent the "Board" no doubt represented the best of diplomacy:

> Office Indian Affairs
> March 7th 1857
>
> Dear Sirs:
>
> I have received your letter of the 4th instant, in which you enquire if the proposal of your Board to establish a school in the Blackfeet Country has been acted upon by the Secretary of the Interior. I have just been up in the Interior Dept. and learned, informally, that the Secretary had the matter up, but finally determined to let it lay over for the decision of his successor.
>
> Yours truly & respectfully,
> Your, & c.
> Charles E. Mix [210]

It was an election year, with Buchanan's turbulent four years about to commence. Nonetheless as we have seen, the 1857 report on the Blackfoot mission hinges the whole enterprise on a government "appropriation for this purpose," prospect of money. (Oh ye of little faith ?) " Until this has been acted upon, no further measures will be adopted for carrying on the mission."[211]

If the Interior Department had given their final approval to the Blackfoot Mission, what would it have looked like? We have a good idea, because the Foreign Board had received similar grants and permissions from the "Department" for other of their Indian missions. The contract for the Sac & Fox Mission, written in 1854 reads like this:

---

[210] Klett, "Missionary Endeavors"

[211] Minutes of the Gen. Assy. of the Pres. Church in the USA. v 15 (1857), Board of Foreign Missions, pp.26-7

This Indenture made and entered into this twenty-second day of November in the year one thousand eight hundred and fifty-four between George W. Commissioner of Indian Affairs on behalf of the Sacs and Foxes of Missouri of the first part and the Board of Foreign Missions of the Presbyterian Church by Walter Lowrie duly authorized thereunto of the second part Witnesseth: That whereas by a treaty made with said Indians on the eighteenth day of May one thousand eight hundred fifty-four the president of the United States is empowered to apply certain funds in such manner as he may deem best for the interest of the said Indians and whereas the said party of the second party (sic) has made certain propositions to educate their children.

Now therefore this Indenture witnesseth that the aforesaid party of the second part agrees to receive into the "boarding school existing on the late Ioway purchase" so many scholars of both sexes as the party of the first part may require to be taken and stipulates to teach them a good English education and in addition to teach the boys farming, the use of tools and agricultural implements, and the girls the various branches of housewifery, including sewing, knitting, and dairy operations and whatever else may tend to advance them in civilization.

The said party of the second part also agrees to take good care of the scholars, so received, to furnish them with good clothing, board, medicine and medical attendance, books and stationary (sic), and to keep them for such length of time as the Secretary of the Interior may prescribe, and report half yearly the number of scholars, their progress, and the condition of the school generally, and to carry out all instructions, not inconsistent with these stipulations, from the Department.

And the party of the first part in behalf of the Sacs and Foxes of Missouri, in consideration hereof and of the premises as aforesaid, agrees to pay to the party of the second part, in half yearly payments commencing from the first day of January one thousand eight hundred and fifty-five, per annum, one thousand five hundred dollars for any number of Scholars not exceeding twenty and in like payments, an allowance of seventy-five dollars per annum, for every scholar above the number of twenty.

And it is distinctly understood and agreed that the power is reserved in the Department to annul this contract at any time, when, in its opinion, the interest of the Indians requires it, and the party of the second part is to be entitled to nothing for any damage that may result therefrom.

In testimony whereof they have hereunto set their hands and seals the day and year first written above.

Geo W. Walter Lowrie
Executed in the presence of
Alfred Chapman[212]

Michael ("Simpson") Culbertson (having been replaced by Walter Lowrie's son Reuben in the China field was home and on the Indian mission committee of the Foreign Missions Board in May 1857. He must have been one of the authors of their report cited early in this book, which mentions Alexander as the originator of the call for the Blackfoot Mission.

In what seems to have been the last gasp of the Mackey mission effort, Lowrie was to write to Alexander again attempting to tie up loose ends of that short-lived Blackfoot mission:

Mission House
New York April 27/57

---

[212] Contract for Mission School for Sacs and Foxes, between Indian Department and Foreign Board, 1854, Presbyterian Historical Society, Indians Mission Correspondence.

Alexr Culbertson Esqr

My Dear Sir

A note this morning from your brother Simpson informs me that you expect to leave St. Louis on the 5th May, for the mountains. We have not given up the Blackfoot mission but are waiting for the decision of the Department to a proposal we have made to them. as we have not received their answer, we can do nothing till next spring. In the mean time we have some supplies & stores there, which may be injured by a delay of another year. If you could sell these for us, you would greatly oblige us. They are—

1 sack coffee 162 lbs @ 11 ½ cts …

1 " dry peaches…

½ bbl Rice 50 @ 12 ½…

10 gal vinegar @ 10. keg 1.00 (?) …

4bbls flour 5 …

2 " pilot (?) bread 3 …

2 " sugar. 572 lbs @ 8 ¾ …

½ " Molas. 22 gal @ 55. …

36 yds carpet. @ 45. … [the letter includes calculations of totals and freight for each item. Grand totals are $124.80 and 2247 lbs.]

The above are the prices which we paid, besides nine cents per lb. for freight. I do not know that you can make any allowance for the freight. If you can allow us eight cents a lb for the freight, we would like to sell all the above articles. But if you cannot make an allowance for the freight, then we would prefer to retain them and take the chance of their being injured during the year. The other articles may remain, & we regret that they must to some extent be in your way. But the delay on the part of the Department has delayed us for this year, though I cannot think they will reject the offer we have made, to establish a mission and farm among this interesting people.

With best wishes, I am Dear Sir,

Yours with sincere regard,

Walter Lowrie [213]

But what of the Mackeys? The January 1857 issue of *The Foreign Missionary* contains a reiterative summary of Elkanah's Report to the Board:

> Mr. Mackey reports his return with his wife, from the Blackfeet Mission, on account of Mrs. Mackeys' health. She had suffered severely from disease, and it was at length necessary to decide on returning home, though Mr. Mackey hopes he will be able to go back next spring. ...The very heavy expense of erecting a dwelling and school-house, at such a distance from the usual means of building, is a serious difficulty. ...[214]

Plaque on pulpit presented to Snow Hill church by Jane Mackey Kelso in memory of her two brothers Elkanah and William, both of whom ministered there.

---

213 Walter Lowrie, LTR, to Alexander Culbertson, April 27, 1857

214 *The Foreign Missionary*, January 1857, p. 266

CHAPTER SIX - The End of the Mission

On April 14, 1857, Elkanah attended a meeting of the Presbytery of New Castle, again. They seem to have kept him occupied until the Fall. When that body met again on October 6:

> The Rev. Elkanah D. Mackey presented a request to be dismissed, in order to connect himself with the Presbytery of Baltimore (as he has received a call from the churches of Snow Hill, and Pitts Creek in their bounds) which request was granted and the stated clerk was directed to furnish him the necessary testimonials. .[215]

Apparently Elkanah and Sarah moved and/or settled near the Maryland churches he was to serve. At a guess, based on the address he gave Lowrie, they had probably been living with relatives in New London, ?Lancaster Co., PA. Elkanah was "received" by the Presbytery of Baltimore at their meeting October 14:

> On Motion the Revd. E. D. Mackay (sic) of the Pres. of New Castle & the Revd. Jas. G. Hamner of the Pres. of the District of Columbia being present were invited to sit as corresponding Members.
>
> Mr. Mackey presented a dismissal from the Pres. of N. Castle to unite with this body & after satisfactory examination they were both received & their names ordered to be enrolled.[216]

---

[215] Reports, Presbytery of New Castle

[216] Minutes, Presbytery of Baltimore, 1854-1866, pp213-214, MSS, PHS (hereafter: Minutes, Baltimore)

On October 15 the churches of Snow Hill and Pitts Creek "placed in his hands" Elkanah's "call" and arrangements were made for his installation as their pastor:

> A call, from the churches of Snow Hill & Pitts Creek for the Pastoral services of the Revd. Elkanah D. Mackay (sic) was presented & read & being found in order was placed in his hands. On his declaring his acceptance thereof Wednesday & Thursday – 29 & 30 December next was fixed as the time of his installation. The Revd. Jos. T. Smith to preside, preach the Sermon & propose the constitutional questions – the Revd. J. H. Kaufman to deliver the charge to the people – Revd. L(?) A. Lefevre his alternate.[217]

He is mentioned in the Presbytery Minutes of October 23, 1857 and April 6, 1858. [218] At the latter meeting a motion was made to "overture" the General Assembly to form a new presbytery of some of the Eastern Shore churches, including Snow Hill and Pitts Creek, which was acted upon, and a Presbytery of Lewes was established.[219] The Minutes of the same meeting affirm Elkanah's installation as pastor of Snow Hill and Pitts Creek. He served these congregations and one at New Town (aka: Newtown) from October 1857 to September 6, 1858. On the later date, two years less one day from the Sunday Agent Hatch claimed he "did not preach" in Fort Benton, he attended a "sacramental" meeting in Princess Anne and "whilst assisting the Rev. A. C. Heaton, . . . during a communion season, he was seized with the

---

[217] ibid, pp 228-229

[218] ibid, pp 232, 251, 253

[219] ibid pp. 262-263; 272-273

malignant bilious fever of which he died. . ." [220] at the age of twenty-eight.

Elkanah's body was buried in the graveyard adjoining the Snow Hill church (now Makemie Memorial Church) in which graveyard two of General Washington's staff are also buried. [221]

A. C. Heaton sent the following article to the *Presbyterian* newspaper "in great haste" four days later:

For the Presbyterian
MELANCHOLY INTELLIGENCE
Princess, Anne, Somerset county, Md.
September 10, 1858

> Messrs. Editors – It is my painful duty to announce to you the death of the Rev. Elkanah D. Mackey, the pastor of the churches at Snow Hill, Pitts Creek, and Newtown. This melancholy event occurred in this place on Monday night last, the 6th inst., at a quarter past eleven o'clock. His disease was a violent type of typhoid fever, induced, in all human probability, by too intense devotion to his labours, and too hazardous exposure of himself. He was here in attendance upon a sacramental meeting when he was taken; and, from the first, his illness was so severe that his removal to his family was impossible. …[222]

Part of a eulogy from another source reads, "His brief career gave evidence of faithfulness and earnestness, being noted for his activity and zeal in the Master's cause, and he was rapidly gaining the affection of the people in his charge."[223]

---

[220] P. H. Almanac, '59-'60, p. 74
[221] North, *Historic Church*
[222] A. C. Heaton, article, dated September 10, in *The Presbyterian*, September 18, 1858.
[223] P. H. Almanac, '59-'60, p. 74

When the new Presbytery of Lewes met, their second motion was to remember him:

> On motion it was resolved, that a committee of two be appointed, in addition to the Moderator [A. C. Heaton] as Chairman, to prepare a tribute to the memory of the Rev. Elkanah Dare Mackey, recently deceased to be published in the Presbyterian. Mssrs Handy & Jones were appointed to this committee.[224]

Elkanah's other memorial left to the young missionary wife did not long outlast the father:

> ...And what renders this calamity [Elkanah's death] more aggravating is the fact that his only child was taken sick a few hours after the father, and died in a few hours after he expired. Thus has fallen, in the prime of life, with the harness on, one of the most promising, energetic, faithful, and devoted young ministers of our denomination. He was in some respects a rare man. His untimely death is a calamity, not only to his family and his circle of relative, but to the churches over which he was placed as watchman, and to the kingdom of God in this vicinity. ...[225]

And yet another account:

> . . .his child died at the manse within twenty-four hours [of his death] and both are buried in the church-yard of the Snow Hill church, the congregation at Princess Anne uniting with that of Snow Hill in erecting a tombstone over the remains. [226]

---

224 Minutes, Presbytery of Lewes, PCUSA, vol 3. , 1858-1870, p. 2
225 A. C. Heaton, article, dated September 10, in *The Presbyterian*, September 18, 1858
226 North, *Historic Church*

Thus ended two lives and the brief ministry of the first Protestant missionaries to the Blackfoots. Thus also dissolved the family of the first white woman on the Upper Missouri. One can hardly help asking what might have been, had they stayed at Fort Benton the winter of 1856-7.

Many years later, Elkanah's sister, Mrs. Jane Kelso of Baltimore, gave a pulpit to the Snow Hill church in memory of Elkanah and William, his brother, who succeeded him as pastor of the three churches, and continued in that office until 1868.[227]

Amidst his other responsibilities, Walter Lowrie was persevering in his attempts to recoup some of the losses to the Presbyterian Board of Foreign Missions, thus six months later this letter was sent:

> Mission House
> New York April 19,1859
> Alexander Culbertson, Esq
> Near Peoria, Ill.
> Dear Sir
>
> Two years ago I sent you a list of articles which had been left at Fort Benton for the Blackfeet mission, and which I requested that you would kindly dispose of for us. Last year on your visit to New York, you informed me that you had disposed of the articles, and the proceeds were in the Establishment in St. Louis. I called at the Country House in May last, but the gentlemen there could not find the entry, on the books.
>
> The Department at Washington seem not much prepared to establish a boarding school among the Blackfeet, such as we proposed. Two years ago, the Secretary of the Interior then in office, referred the question to his Successor, and the subject has not been taken up by him. In these circumstances we have reluctantly concluded to give up this mission, at least for

[227] North, *Historic Church*

the present. We would now be glad to dispose of all the stores we have at Fort Benton & Fort Union, at cost, and at such allowance for freight as the Fur Company may deem reasonable, under the circumstance. If you could undertake charge of this matter for us, we would be greatly obliged. I will in that case send you the original receipts, giving a list of the articles, freight & c. Please let me hear from you in regard to this matter, & with best wishes & regard

I am sincerely W. L.[228]

To which A. Culbertson replied:

Walter Lowrie Esqr

New York City

Dear Sir

Yours of the 19th on the subject of Merchandise & c belonging the Mission was duly recd.

I leave this for St. Louis on the 26th when it will afford me pleasure to attend to the matter and see that everything is right.

I think however the Gentlemen on the Upper Missouri (?Mission) have not sent to St. Louis an act. of the property in which even we will not be able to get a correct act. until the return of our Anual Boat in Agust.

I am sorry you [have] given up the establishment of a Mission amongst the Blkfeet alltho I scarcely ever expect to Visit them again I still feel an interest in their future welfare.

Very respectfully Truly

Yours & c. Alexr Culbertson[229]

Alexr Culbertson

---

[228] Klett, "Missionary Endeavors"

[229] ibid

The last letter extant about the Mackey Mission to the Blackfeet was written by Walter Lowrie :

Mission House
New York April 27, 1859

Alexr Culbertson Esq.

Dear Sir

I have your favor of the 23r instant, and we are greatly obliged by your kind offer to take charge of the transfer of the articles we have at Fort Benton, and Fort Union. I send herewith the receipt of the articles left at those places, and a list of the articles as far as we have an account of them. It will be a great favor to us, if the Fur Company will purchase them, as the cost of bringing them back would in some cases be more than they are worth. The article of freight we leave entirely to the company. We shall be satisfied with any decision they may make. Light articles in the boxes, not wanted, may be sent back, with the box of school books. One article is a side saddle which I presume is not wanted at Fort Benton. The articles returned, may be sent to Mr. Joseph G. Miller in St. Louis, our agent there.

Respectfully & Truly Yours
WL[230]

No, the side saddle was not needed. However, according to John Canfield Ewers, Elkanah Mackey's "advent was long remembered by the Blackfeet, primarily because he brought his wife with him."[231]

---

[230] ibid

[231] John Canfield Ewers, *The Blackfeet: Raiders on the Northwestern Plains*, 1958

64 64

Mission House
New York April 27. 1859

Alext Culbertson Esq
Dear Sir

I have your favor of the 23rd instant, and we are greatly obliged by your kind offer to take charge of the transfer of the articles we have at Fort Benton, and Fort [illegible]. I send herewith the receipt of the articles left at those places, and a list of the articles as far as we have an account of them. It will be a great favor to us, if the Fur Company will purchase them from us, as the cost of carrying them back, would in some cases be more than they are worth. The articles of freight we leave entirely to the company. We shall be satisfied with any decision they may make. Light articles as the books, not wanted, may be sent back, with the box of school books. One article is a side saddle which I presume is not wanted at Fort Benton. The articles returned, may be sent to Mr Joseph [illegible] in St Louis, our agent there.

Respectfully & truly Yours
W L

Walter Lowrie's last letter to Alexander Culbertson

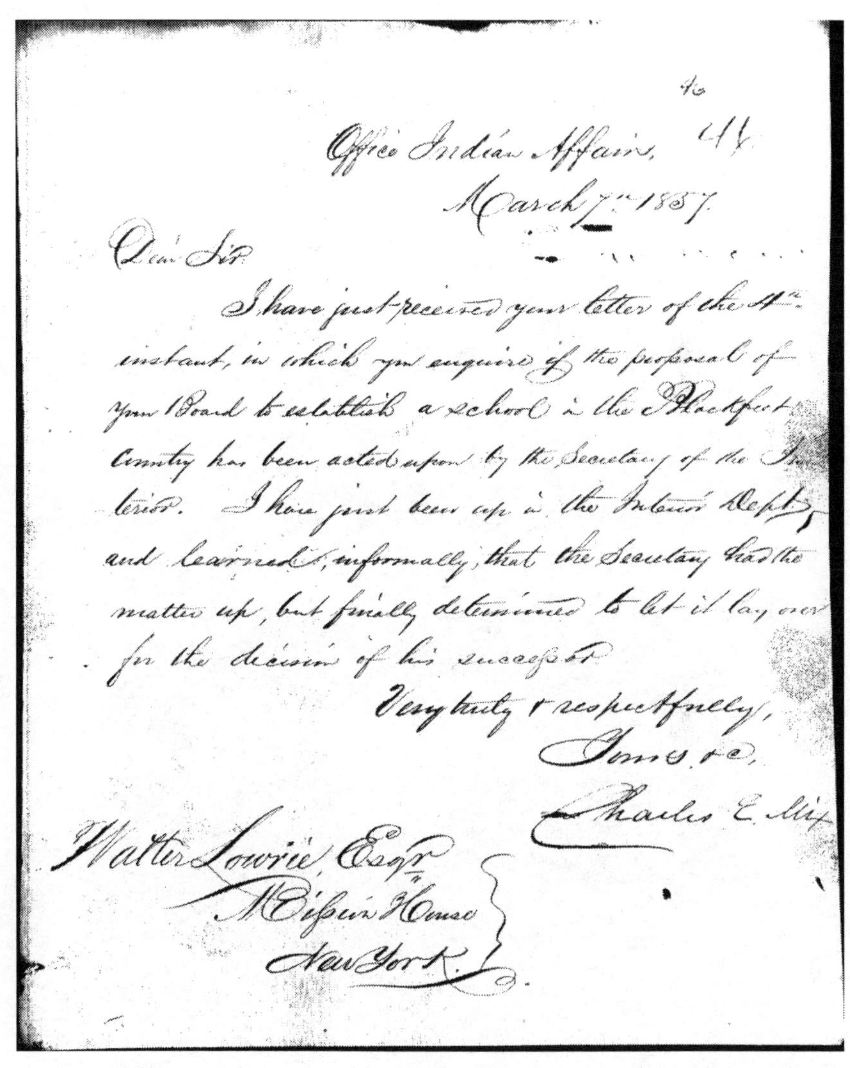

46

Office Indian Affairs,

March 7th 1857.

Dear Sir:

I have just received your letter of the 4th instant, in which you enquire if the proposal of your Board to establish a school in the Blackfeet Country has been acted upon by the Secretary of the Interior. I have just been up in the Interior Dept., and learned, informally, that the Secretary had the matter up, but finally determined to let it lay over for the decision of his successor.

Very truly & respectfully,

Yours &c.

Charles E. Mix

Walter Lowrie, Esqr.

Mission House

New York.

Office of Indian Affairs 1857 letter to Walter Lowrie concerning delay in decision about Blackfoot school

From a photo of Alexander Culbertson

CHAPTER SEVEN - What Might Have Been

What might have come of the Blackfoot Mission if the Mackeys had chosen to remain through that long, hard winter in Montana? While lengthy pursuit of such a subject belongs more properly to a work of fiction, some implications of their departure and the abrupt end of the mission might be pointed out here.

Had they stayed and secured more help, they would most likely have built a mission and school either to the southwest or northwest of Fort Benton. The site that sounds most favorable in the Report is likely Highwood creek, perhaps about where the town of Highwood is today. However the 1855 Stevens Treaty indicated the Blackfoot's land were to be north of the Missouri, and Highwood is south of it. Agent Vaughan and others settled on the Sun River region for their marginally successful agricultural experiments among the Blackfoots. How a Presbyterian school might have worked out is hard to say.

They would have had six years in which to establish stable relations with the Blackfoot tribes - before the great influx of gold seekers which came in 1862. Those six years, moreover, were the peak of good relations between the Blackfoot nation and white Americans.

Those relations had historically been poor. The Blackfoots had some dealings with Europeans as far back as the Verendryes (ca 1740) and perhaps earlier during raids into the Southwest for horses. There was some contact with British explorers and traders before 1800 (Alexander Henry in 1775 and Peter Pond in 1785). In the first decades of the nineteenth century the Blackfoots established regular if minimal relations with Hudson Bay Company.

The first recorded encounter between Americans and Blackfoots took place when Meriwether Lewis went into the heart of Blackfoot country hoping to find a Northwest passage near the sources of Maria's (now the Marias) River. Returning disappointed, in July 1806, Lewis and one of his men killed two Piegans after an altercation. This became the pattern for American-Blackfoot relations over the next quarter of a century.

In 1807, John Colter and a party of Crows had another brush with Blackfoots near the Three Forks of the Missouri and in 1808, Colter and John Potts ran into Blackfoots again, resulting in Pott's death and Colter's famous run. In the fall of 1809, Andrew Henry and company, Manuel Lisa's men, went with Colter to set up a post at Three Forks. The Blackfoots killed more than twenty of their trappers and the post was abandoned.

Other white interlopers were killed in 1822 (Andrew Henry, again with an Ashley-Henry post on the Yellowstone), 1823 (Missouri Fur Company men killed on the Yellowstone) and in 1828 (Sublette trading party on Birch Creek). The Blackfoots were predisposed to expect aggression and violence from the American trappers and to give back as good or better than they got.

It was therefore a bold act for Jacob Berger, serving with Alexander McKenzie of American Fur Company, to go from old Fort Union up the Marias River to Badger Creek to make peace with the Blackfoots in 1829. The trader, who had learned the Blackfoot language in Canada, spent the winter with the Blackfoots and, in 1830, led a party of Piegans back down to Fort Union for a council with McKenzie, resulting in a treaty which was the beginning of a long-standing friendship between

American Fur Company and the Blackfoots, particularly the Piegan branch.

Apart from set-backs in 1832, when a party of Bloods caused Fort Piegan, at the mouth of the Marias, to be abandoned, and a year of hostility due to the short tempers of F. A. Chardon and Alexander Harvey in 1843-44, the peace between American Fur posts and the Blackfoots continued until the 1860's.

Alexander Culbertson took over Fort McKenzie in 1833, and became a good friend of the Blackfoots. That he took a Blackfoot wife shows something of his feelings for that tribe and further cemented the bond of peace. He warned the Indians of smallpox danger in 1837, but they contracted it from goods, nonetheless – and nearly six thousand died in the epidemic of 1837-38.

After Alexander Harvey's year of hostility (1843-44), Culbertson, who had been transferred elsewhere (to Fort Laramie, where he learned adobe building), returned and re-established good relations again. He began to build Fort Benton in 1846 and officially completed it the next year (although as we have said, the rebuilding of the Fort in adobe, took place gradually over a number of years beginning in 1850) . The fort was named for Senator Benton of Missouri whose political machinations rescued American Fur from jeopardy when they were caught manufacturing and selling liquor to the Indians. The "friendship" of American Fur never precluded trading in firearms and alcohol, in fact at times they seemed to be central to it. Wiser traders, however, were careful with the latter.

In 1851 Culbertson brought the first wagon overland from Fort Union to Fort Benton (essentially the same route the Mackeys were to travel with him five years later.). In 1853 he introduced Isaac Stevens, the government commissioner, to the Blackfoot chiefs. In 1855, Stevens held a council near the mouth of the Judith

River, where he negotiated a treaty with the Blackfoots as well as chiefs from many of the other tribes of the Northwest Plains. That treaty was relatively generous, both in terms of annuities and facilities promised as well as in lands set aside for the Blackfoots. When Agent Hatch brought the year's annuities up in 1856, it seemed to the Blackfoots a hopeful sign of American faithfulness.

Holterman tells us that during 1856, on a visit to the Catholic mission at St. Ignatius, Little Dog told the priests there, "The traders never speak to us of God." How poignant that expression of Blackfoot spiritual hunger. How poignant that failure, joined to the failure of the Presbyterian mission.

In retrospect, everything might be said to appear as though orchestrated for the Mackeys arrival. They had or would have had six years in which to establish a mission, a school, perhaps a strong Blackfoot church and good personal relationships with the Blackfoots in general.

Furthermore with Walter Lowrie and Alexander Culbertson firmly behind them, the Mackeys would have been in a strong position to exert political influence on behalf of the people they served. They might have helped maintain a regular delivery of the annuities, the non-delivery of which was one thing that soured relations over the following decade. They might have defended the Blackfoot's Treaty rights to lands, which the gold-hungry and "manifest destiny" minded, white intruders rapidly encroached upon. At least they might have pushed for the ratification of the (less generous) 1865 and 1868 treaties and the maintenance of their provisions. They might have taught agriculture as a respectable option to the Blackfoots before the extinction of the buffalo overtook them.

In fact what happened during the period from the discovery of gold at Grasshopper Creek in 1862 up to the Starvation Winter of 1883 was the reversal of all the improvements in Blackfoot relations from 1829 to 1862.

Gold-seekers from the East flocked up the river headed for the diggings in the vicinity of the present Helena (capital of Montana), They had no respect for Indians or Indian treaties – no more than the freighters who began to do booming business driving their mule and ox trains between Benton and the diggings. The Blackfoots, and the Bloods in particular, retaliated by raiding the trains.

During the 1864-5 "Sun River Stampede" into Blackfoot lands, whites shot one Piegan and hanged three others, despite the fact that Little Dog[232] of the tribe had saved the lives of a number of stranded and starving miners that winter. There was an armed reprisal by the Blackfoots which resulted in one death and the closure of the government farm at Sun River.

Starting in the spring of 1865, Blackfoots raided regularly around the settlement of Fort Benton, while whites took bloody revenge upon any Blackfoot who ventured into town. A treaty council in 1865 was accounted a fiasco. Another in 1868 seemed to do little, since it was never ratified.

Holterman describes some of the violence in Fort Benton against Indians at that time:

> . . .When a couple of night herders were slain by Crows, probably by a passing war-party, vigilantes or Bentonites turned upon all the Indians they could lay hands on. When three Blackfeet appeared in town, they were lynched. These may be the three that young Joe [Culbertson, Alexanders son] discovered when he and a

---

[232] Little Dog, who became head chief of the Piegan Blackfoots when Lame Bull died in 1857, was a remarkably wise and tolerant leader and worked to build peaceful relationships with the white interlopers. He himself joined in after the government farm was established on Sun River. He was instrumental in bringing together the Indians for the Stevens Treaty Council in 1855, and did much else for the white traders, etc. He was killed, probably by fellow tribesmen, in 1866. (Holterman, "Little Dog")

> friend were taking a morning ride on the edge of town. The three corpses were hanging from a pole scaffolding with a note pinned onto the shirt of one: "These are three good Indians." A few days later, according to Joe's personal notes, a Blood Indian came down from the Whoop-up country and "stopped at our house." A man named George stormed into the house, seized the Blood, dragged him outside and shot him. . . the body of this lone Indian was thrown into a well .[233]

The exchange of bloodletting continued to its peak when 56 whites were killed in 1869, including the influential Malcolm Clarke, who may have been killed by his Piegan in-laws. The awful conclusion came in January 1870, when Major Eugene Baker's troops killed 173 Piegans on the Marias River – by mistake. The "Baker Massacre," as it is quite accurately called, occurred when Baker set out on a supposed surprise raid against Mountain Chief's hostile band, but instead attacked the small-pox ridden and thoroughly friendly band of Heavy Runner, killing women and children as well as the aged Heavy Runner, himself. Always the innocent for our sins. This massacre was the last major act of white-Blackfoot warfare, though it can hardly be said to have reestablished friendly relations between the two peoples.

Neither did the Culbertson family escape the growing alienation between white and Blackfoot. Jack Holterman tells us of the last record of the intact family before their compounded sorrows split it apart:

> The U.S. Census for 1870 lists the Culbertsons as if they were still the first family of Fort Benton and Chouteau County, as if indeed, they formed an island of domestic tranquility in this ocean of discord and bloodletting: Alex (sic) Culbertson, trader, age 61; Natawista, "keeps

[233] Holterman, *King of the High Missouri*, p. 172

house", age 45; Fannie, at home, age 20; Joseph, at home, age 12; Robert, clerk in the store, age 27. [234]

But Holterman goes on to tell us of the event of which Joseph Culbertson later said, "the tears drop out of my eyes as I write this story to you. That was the downfall of my dear old father."[235]

Natawista Culbertson, circa 1859, from *Frontier Diplomats*, by permission of her descendants, the Taylor Family

[234] Holterman, *King of the High Missouri*, p. 176
[235] Holterman, p. 177

> One day, probably not long after this count was taken, Natawista was gone. . . .the Kaina princess who had sampled every phase of the white American way of life, had lived through the Civil War, had risen to the glamour of social success and endured racism and the collapse of a fortune – at last she had enough. Her reasons? We can only guess: the January carnage on the Marias, the corpse in the well, news of the death of her brother Seen-From-Afar . . .Perhaps this was the last straw.
>
> Joe learned that his mother had disappeared, probably in the caravan of trader John Replinger headed up the Marias. For Joe, it was a trauma he never quite recovered from. For Natawista it was the return to her people in their season of grief and ultimate defeat.[236]

There was much more suffering ahead of the Blackfoots. Soon the buffalo – those herds stretching as far as Sarah Mackey's eyes could see -- were gone and that suddenly – so that some witnesses spoke of them being "swallowed up" by the earth. In 1883, without receiving the promised annuities and in extreme need of supplies, the Blackfoots on their much reduced reservation suffered terrible losses from starvation. The Agent at the time was a Methodist minister, established there under President Grant's "peace policy". Although that policy gave the Methodists control of affairs for the Blackfoot reservation,[237] it did little to provide education or prosperity, much less a credible offer of Christian hope. The Catholics maintained a more consistent presence, yet

[236] Holterman, p. 176

[237] Grant's Peace Policy officially designated major church denominations as agents for particular tribes and reservations around the United States. That's one of many historical indications that "separation of church and state" as discussed in our times , is an innovation.

neither were they able to help the Blackfoots much, either in positive provision, or in resisting white sin patterns.

Presbyterians remained few and far between in the territory. A Rev. George Smith came to the diggings at Bannack in 1864, and apparently was later in Virginia City.[238]

Curiously the Presbyterians finally tried to re-establish a presence in 1912, with a Rev. James D. Gold, who remained in Browning on the Blackfoot reservation, until 1926. During that time, the Presbyterian congregation is said to have been, for the most part, composed of whites working on the reservation. It

---

[238] Hal Stearns, "'Best of the good'brought Christianity to frontiersmen,." *Great Falls Tribune* article, October 5,1985, p. 4-A.

See also: *The Pioneer Work of the Presbyterian Church in Montana,* ed. Geo. Edwards, p 14, "Sketch of the Beginning of Presbyterianism in Montana, " by Rev. Thomas V. Moore, D.D. which includes this passage: "The work of the Rev. George Grantman Smith marks the real beginning of Presbyterian Missions in Montana. Mr. Smith a member of Third Presbytery of Philadelphia, a graduate of Princeton College and Auburn Theological Seminary, was sent out by the Presbyterian Committee of Home Missions (New School) of which Dr. Kendall was the secretary, as the first regularly commissioned Protestant missionary for Montana. Mr. Smith intended to go to Gaboon, Africa, but finding that it was easier for the Board to get missionaries for West Africa than for Montana, he chose the latter field."

Smith was born 31 Jan 1833, in Philadelphia; graduated from Princeton in 1861; was licensed by Third Presbytery, appointed a chaplain in the G. A. R., after which he went to Auburn Seminary; and was ordained in May 1864, whereupon he went out at once to Montana. He reached Bannack (present Helena area) in June 1864. "In 1866, on his return to the east, he married Miss Anna M. Swift, in New Jersey," and preached in a mission chapel in Buffalo, New York, for about six years. Smith wrote, "I left Montana in 1866, passed through Helena on the way to Fort Benton, and down the Missouri to the states." (*Letters*, Smith to Rev. Thos. V. Moore, 1897.)

(See also: *M. H. S. Contributions,* Vol 6, 1907, pp.293-4)

"included all the 'prominent' [white] people of Browning," by the 1920's.

Elkanah D. Mackey first appears in this account writing to the Mission about a tombstone, so perhaps it is fitting to make some last reference to his own.

The historical pamphlet concerning Makemie Memorial Church, Snow Hill, MD, by Mary North indicates that Elkanah's grave was in the graveyard of that church. The original building was of logs and stood near the Pocomoke river. The second building was a frame structure about fifty yards from the present one, and collapsed, whereupon a brick structure was erected on the same spot. This became the building where Elkanah ministered. The present building was constructed in 1887, and dedicated in 1890. I visited there in 1984.

The minister, Rev. Holsey, drove up to the church just as I had begun looking through the graveyard. He rather took the wind out of my sails by saying he had looked the graveyard over pretty thoroughly and never seen Elkanah's grave marker. He suggested a number of graves were disturbed when a new addition was built, and stones moved, some of them ending up leaning against the wall of a basement room. He kindly guided me around however, showing me the memorial plaque for the pulpit. He also showed me the stones in the basement, although we found none for Mackeys.

After departing somewhat crestfallen, I took care of the business of our accommodations, but decided to come back and search the graveyard one more time. Much to my surprise and joy, I indeed found the rather conspicuous marker. It was inscribed both for Elkanah and his daughter[239] – not a headstone but a sort of table -

---

[239] Holterman, p. 128, speaks incorrectly, of Elkanah's "son" dying soon after him and buried in the same graveyard. Leslie

arrangement, a dark stone slab lying horizontal not quite at waist height, laid on a marble base -- sort of a pseudo-crypt. All the lettering except the maker's name was still legible.

Elkanah and Julie Anna Mackey Table-tomb, Makemie Memorial Church, Snow Hill, MD

It was located not far from the northwest corner of the present building which would have been southwest of the building then standing. It is between the stones of one Selby N. Johnson and a small stone marked Ida Jane Mackey, daughter of brother William[240] and Laura W.

Wischmann repeats this in her book. Mea culpa. This was misinformation Holterman got from me. I first saw the grave and its inscription a year or so after our correspondence. Prior to that I picked up the idea the child was a boy.

240 William Downing Mackey, 1829-1886, took over the pastorate of the three churches Elkanah was serving at the time of his death. After nine years he moved on for two more years of pastoring, and then became a professor of Ancient Languages at the University of Delaware. He continued to preach "supply" in various churches until the last year of his life.

Mackey. (Ida Jane was Elkanah's niece, born in 1865 and died the next year. Her stone is inscribed, "He shall gather the lambs with his arm and carry them in his bosom.")

This stone over Elkanah's grave reads:

OUR PASTOR
AND
HIS CHILD

REV. ELKANAH DARE MACKEY
Born Sept. 16th, 1836
Died Sept. 6th, 1858

JULIA ANNA
Born Jan. 3rd, 1857
Died Sept. 7th, 1858

Erected by the Congregations of
Snow Hill and Pitts Creek

CHAPTER EIGHT -- The Surviving Widow

What became of Sarah, the surviving member of the Presbyterian Mission to the Blackfoots? One need not be a radical feminist to agree history is notoriously poor at keeping track of women. Over many years I was frustrated by not being able to finish the story, the hanging question being what became of Sarah Armstrong Mackey?

In the days before the internet blossomed, my researches at the Presbyterian Historical Society turned up no further word on Sarah. As the internet began to expand, my inquiries on genealogical sites were not fruitful.

Then in the early 1990s I found a reference online to a portrait photograph of a Sarah Armstrong Mackey, in juxtaposition with two other names: Laura Isabelle Mackey and Richard Guthrie Mackey. That was puzzling. The three were listed with reference numbers in the index of the "Vertical files" of the Maryland Historical Society, in Baltimore.

I knew Sarah had been "of Cecil County, Maryland" at the time of her marriage to Elkanah. But I could not imagine who these other two Mackeys could be – no other reference to Richard Guthrie Mackey was known to me. Likewise Laura. Could they be children? But the obituary in a Presbyterian publication said Elkanah's "only child survived him but a short time, and they were buried together in the same grave."[241]

[241] *Presbyterian Historical Almanac and Annual Remembrancer for the Church, 1860,* Second Vol. Philadelphia, Joseph M. Wilson, 1860. p. 74

I wondered if it were possible Sarah had been pregnant with fraternal twins at the time her husband and first daughter's died. If this was indeed she, who else could these other two be but her children -- because if she had remarried and had more children – her last name wouldn't be Mackey, would it? Thus I convinced myself this was some other family, and I did not pursue it, although I did searches now and again hoping new material would become available.

Then quite recently, I did a casual search, and found the online genealogical website Find-a-Grave had put together some data, sources unknown, indicating a Rev. Richard Guthrie Mackey was not only Sarah Armstrong's second husband, but also Elkanah's brother! Laura Isabelle Mackey (married name Sanner), was said to be their daughter – one of several children born to Sarah's second marriage.

So I decided to hunt down those photographs. Through further inquiries, I found the "vertical files" were references to books in the Maryland Historical Society's possession. But I found through visits and messages in June 2016, that the personnel of the historical society's Special Collection were unable to locate them!

The Find-a-Grave webpage indicated Elkanah's parents, William Mackey (1783 - 1851) and Sarah Mackey (1790 - 1875) had two children beyond the four I'd found in Presbyterian sources. They showed Elkanah's siblings included not only James Love Mackey, William Downing Mackey and Jane Anne Mackey (Kelso), but also Richard Guthrie Mackey (1822 – 1888) and Eliza Mackey Commons (1824 - 1897).

The website showed the widowed Sarah E. Armstrong Mackey marrying Richard Guthrie Mackey, her second husband being Elkanah's to-me previously unknown sibling. Richard was himself a widower, his first wife having been Emley/Emily Baldwin.

Richard and Sarah were shown to have had two more children in addition to three from Richard's first marriage.[242] These first three were said to be: William Ambrose Mackey (1846 – 1868), Sarah E. Mackey Standiford (1847 - ____) and Richard Anthony Mackey (1853 - 1922). The two children of Richard and Sarah were listed as: Laura Isabelle Mackey Sanner (1863 - 1926) and William Kelso Mackey (1869 - 1876).

There were a number of things that made this new information plausible:

A/Richard Guthrie Mackey's middle name is elsewhere shown as the last name of Elkanah's mother's (Sarah Martin Mackey) Scottish grandparents.

B/William Kelso Mackey's middle name is the married name of Elkanah's sister, Jane.

But in the negative column at this point, I noted that under William Kelso Mackey's own entry, Find-a-grave listed Elkanah as father -- impossible since William was born in 1869, ten years after Elkanah's death.

Also Richard Guthrie Mackey was listed as a "Rev." but extensive online research turned up no record of him. Mt. Zion Methodist church where his grave is, seems to have been a United Brethren church at its inception, possibly becoming an Evangelical United Brethren Church before uniting with the Methodists to form the United Methodist church. [243]

Finally casting doubt on the new information was the fact that all the biographical records of Elkanah, and the Mackey family of Union Presbyterian Church (Kirkwood/ Coleraine) mention <u>three</u> brothers – not four. However, looking more closely, I find the obituary/ memorial for James Love Mackey, who died in 1867 says:

---

[242] There turned out to be six children from his first marriage.

[243]The United Brethren were one of the first "non-denominational" churches.

"He leaves behind him a mother, brothers, sisters, and a bereaved widow. . ."[244] Since Elkanah had been dead for many years, "brothers" indicates there were more than just William surviving the two of them. Furthermore "sisters" indicates at least one other sister beside Jane (Kelso). However, I also knew older usage sometimes labeled in-laws as brother or sister.

There was a Mackey family genealogy book I had heard of back in the 1980's – and indeed I had corresponded with the compiler: *Some Mackey Settlers Along the Mason-Dixon Line* by Anne G. Copley. She had written: " My book has quite a lot about Elkanah Mackey and family. It is for sale for $38.00 postage paid. If you are interested e-mail me."

Money was pretty tight then, and I tried negotiate a lesser fee for the info on Elkanah – nothing doing! More recently, as I got going on the project again, I was ready to spend the money, but could not find a copy for sale!

However, while searching for that book online, I learned of yet another Mackey genealogy book, *The Mackey Family, 1729-1975,* published in 1974 by Wilmer Mackey Sanner. His last name tied in to the Find-A-Grave data, and so I girded my loins and bought a copy online -- spending considerably more than Ms. Copley had asked for hers!

But the results so far exceeded my fondest hopes, that I would gladly have paid twice as much for Mr. Sanner's book . Not only did it affirm most of what was posted on Find-a-Grave, it added vastly to the information about Sarah's second marriage to Elkanah's brother Richard Guthrie Mackey. The book also corrected a few things, such as the fact Richard was NOT a minister and thus didn't show up in any denominational records. But

---

[244] Thus in two sources, one no doubt quoting the other: *Presbyterian Historical Almanac and Annual Remembrancer of the Church.* 1867.

much to my joy, the book also contained photographs of all three, Elkanah, Sarah, and Richard !

Finally, gloriously beyond that, it also contained a typescript of Sarah's 1856 Diary which I did not even know existed until then, as well as the supplemental Journal entries by Elkanah from their mission trip! And after my more than 30 years of asking, this book gave the answers to what became of the amazing lady, the first American of European extraction to venture as far up the Missouri as my home town, a mere hundred and sixty years ago.

Elkanah died September 6, 1858. Their daughter, Julia Anna died the next day, September 7, 1858.[245] Sarah had hardly been in Snow Hill long enough to make many friends. Her loved ones - and Elkanah's - were up in Cecil Co., Maryland, and Lancaster Co., Pennsylvania. She likely put her affairs in order, and went back home.

It's true, her brother-in-law William Downey Mackey [246] took up the mantle of the Snow Hill ministry, so he and his wife, Laura Pitts Mackey may have provided some measure of comfort to her, indeed this may be part of why she named her next daughter Laura. But it seems another of Elkanah's brothers was destined to become her greatest human comforter.

Richard Guthrie Mackey, four years older than Elkanah, had lost his first wife, Emley Baldwin, somewhere between the birth of their youngest daughter, Serena Jane, in April 1857 and 1861. Not much is known about Emily Baldwin, but Richard and Elkanah's sister, Jane Kelso, mentions the death of her "sister-in-law Emley

---

[245] These are the death dates engraved on the table stone over their grave in Makemie Memorial Churchyard Cemetery, in Snow Hill, MD.
[246] Wm. D. Mackey became one of the founders of Delaware College, now the University of Delaware, and ministered for many years at White Clay Presbyterian church, of which he wrote a history.

Baldwin, wife of my brother Richard Guthrie Mackey" in her will.

We know nothing about their "courtship," but Richard and Sarah were married 13 February, 1862.

Sarah inherited not just three, but six children from the ages of three to seventeen- three boys and three girls, formerly her nieces and nephews. They were Samuel, William, Sarah, Eliza, Richard and Serena.

Richard Guthrie Mackey, Elkanah'a brother and Sarah's second husband

Fourteen months later, she delivered another daughter to the crew, Laura Isabelle. That was in April 1863.

With her second marriage, Sarah became wife to a energetic lumberman and farmer, whose enterprise and ingenuity allowed him to adapt to unexpected hardships: We know already, that she could handle a fair amount of hardship herself.

> [Richard Guthrie Mackey's] first wife died and his brother Elkanah died, so he married secondly Elkanah's widow, Sarah Elizabeth (Armstrong) Mackey. Not many years later, due to very heavy rain storms, he lost an entire year's lumber crop. Having a good tract of land in Baltimore County, he cut the timber and built a fine home and started farming; then built a cannery to process the produce raised. [247]

The new farm was in the northern part of Baltimore county, just below the Pennsylvania line, near Freeland. Richard and Sarah's next two children were born there.

The farm and cannery employed a number of hands. But their second son, (her step-son) William Ambrose, went off independently, to work for the railroad. Sarah's oldest step-daughter, Sarah Emma, was married in January, 1868, to Adolphus Standiford, and they moved to Baltimore.

The notebook containing Sarah's and Elkanah's 1856 diary and journal has an interesting addendum, four and a half pages written in Sarah's hand when her daughter, Laura, was five or six - about 1868. I quote it in full here, because it contains such a clear expression of Sarah's own faith, despite her considerable vicissitudes. It

---

[247] *The Mackey Family,* Wilmer Mackey Sanner, Second part, page 1

is a record of an affectionate end-of-day dialogue with Laura:

> Oh Mama I have had such a nice time with those dear little girls. I am so sorry they cannot stay longer. But I will have you for my company now, won't I, Mama?
>
> Yes, my little darling come here & I will try to interest you for a short time. Now tell me what your little playmates and you have been doing all this long afternoon.
>
> Why, Mama, we have been doing lots of things. Playing thimble, Hotbutter Beans, poor pussy wants a corner, had meeting, and oh what a nice time we did have singing Oh! how I love Jesus.
>
> I am so glad my little daughter has had such a pleasant time.
>
> That is a beautiful hym and I hope my little Laura will one day fully realize that she does love that blessed Jesus whom we all ought to love, because he first loved us. We should always strive to be on the side of a Jesus. That is the true side.
>
> Mama does that mean we must always tell the truth.
>
> That is not exactly what I ment by the remark. But if we are on the true side we will not have a desire to tell an untruth. And I hope my little darling will ask our Father in Heaven to give her a new heart in the days of her youth and that she may come out desidedly on the Lord's side which is the True side.
>
> There are a great many sides in this world, the "Shady side" "Sunny Side" the inside, the outside, the right side, and the wrong side, the True side and the false side. And I think I promised on one occasion to give you some account of a little girl who was seriously impressed and anxiously inquiering the True way when she was quite young.
>
> Oh tell me, tell me for I love so much to hear about little girls.

> But I fear I have already taxed your little mind too much, as you seem fatigued with your day's play. And it is growing late my little daughter will excuse me with the promis of commencing my story tomorrow.
>
> So after the Necesary preparation little Laura said, "Now I lay me down to sleep I pray the Lord my soul to keep. If I should die before I wake, I pray the Lord my soul to take. God bless Papa, Mama, Brothers, Sisters and every Body. Amen."
>
> And very soon she was sleeping sweetly and by her Bead side kneeling, I asked God to keep her and incline her heart to do that which was right & pleasing in his sight.[248]

But the vicissitudes were not over. That same year a tragic episode came to Richard and Sarah when William, working as a railroad conductor or brakeman, fell between two cars and was killed.

But another son was born in December 1869, and they named him William, too, middle name Kelso – for his married Aunt Jane. Yet once again sorrow came as little Willie only lived until August 1870. They buried his remains near his brother's in the cemetery in Freeland of what is now Zion United Methodist church.[249]

Two years later the last of Richard and Sarah's children, Hattie Edwards, was born, in October 1872, while the following month their Eliza Edith married Joseph S. Freeland, whose family had loaned the community its name. A biography of Joseph makes a point of the fact that although his family were Methodists, his wife, "Edith's" family were Presbyterians with Pennsylvania Scotch-Irish roots.[250]

---

248 The Mackey Family, Wilmer Mackey Sanner.

249 Find-A-Grave shows the family obelisk, one side of which says WM. AMBROSE at the top and WILLIE KELSO at the bottom.

250 *A Biographical History of York County, Pennsylvania,* edited by John Gibson. Clearfield Reprints, 1989, p. 173:

Gradually the rest of the children married and/or moved away until only Laura and Hattie were home.

For a while Laura Isabelle attended McKim's finishing school in Baltimore and stayed with her aunt Jane Kelso at 110 East Baltimore Street while studying there. [251]

The running of the farm and cannery must have been hard work. It may well be that the business had been going downhill for a few years by then. It seems to have been heavily mortgaged. Richard's hard work and ingenuity weren't able to keep ahead of the financial pressures. For all the comfort Sarah was to him and his children, after nearly 26 years of this second marriage, Richard died at the farm on the 1st of January 1888. Laura was 24 years old. Hattie, their youngest child, was fifteen.

In fairly short order, Sarah gave up on the farm and cannery, although Wilmer Mackey Sanner gives her credit for trying:

> Sarah tried to employ people to operate the farm and cannery, but she was not successful. There being no insurance and with a heavy mortgage due, she retired to Philadelphia where she opened a boarding house to support her two [surviving] children. [252]

Within two years of Richard's death, Sarah moved to 4023 Baring Street in Philadelphia, and apparently ran a boarding house there. This is in the Powelton Village section of West Philadelphia, which was at that time experiencing a boom in housing due to the transportation situation.

Sarah Mackey who had travelled great distances via so many modes of transportation during her first year of

---

[251] *The Mackey Family*, Second part, p. 6

[252] ibid, p. 1

marriage, was supporting her second widowhood at a nexus of transportation:

Richard Guthrie Mackey memorial – family obelisk
Zion Methodist Church, Freeland, Baltimore Co., MD

> . . .It could be argued in fact that Powelton Village was the first stop on the Main Line, the stretch of track connecting Philadelphia with Pittsburgh
>
> [It is a] grand suburban development that grew up around the Pennsylvania Railroad's Main Line tracks in the 1890s and early 1900s. Powelton is a hybrid of streetcar and railroad suburban development: for the second half of the nineteenth century, it was serviced by both horse drawn (later electric) streetcars and by Main

> Line trains. The surviving freestanding mansions on Powelton Avenue, Baring Street, and Hamilton Street are large and ornate, yet they are set within walking distance of each other rather than being secluded on larger lots as they were on the Main Line. They are also located within a few minutes walk of the former Powelton Avenue stop. Unlike the Main Line developments, there are also a significant number of twin houses and row house blocks intermingled with the free-standing houses. [253]

4023 Baring is located between Spring Garden and Powelton Avenue about 4 blocks north of 40th and Market.[254]

This was her mother's home, the address from which Laura was married to Rev. George Roberts Sanner, in October of 1889.[255] George was another Marylander from Baltimore. He and Laura were to have five children, the youngest being Wilmer Mackey Sanner, who became the family genealogist.

"G. R. Sanners," as Laura's husband is listed in Methodist records, was the first/founding pastor of Darlington United Methodist Church in Darlington, MD from 1889-1891; and thereafter served in many churches of the Baltimore District. These included East Hartford; Bennett Mem; Elk Ridge; New Hope, Brunswick; Columbia Ave., etcetera.

Laura and Rev. George had their first two children in Darlington and Libertyville, Maryland, in 1890 and 1892. Wilmer was to be born in 1902, at the parsonage in Aberdeen, MD, near the famous military proving ground.

---

253 "Powelton Avenue: The First Stop on the Main Line?" By STEVEN UJIFUSA Published: Jan 26, 2015, the Philly History blog online.

254 Now a completely renovated rental property – 2 units, each with 2 bedrooms, 1 bath – $1300 per month according to online listings.

255 *The Mackey Family,* Part Two, p. 6

Sarah Armstrong Mackey on her 65th birthday

Sarah may have run the boarding house in Philadelphia for five or six years, but her children were having children of their own, and making their own way. It might be argued she deserved a rest.

The youngest, Hattie Edwards, married Alfred Russ Baxter in August 1893. He was from a respected family in Quincy , Massachusetts. (Later Alfred worked in the monument and tombstone business in Trenton, New Jersey.)

It was in Quincy, in August 1894, that Hattie and Alfred produced their only child, although they named him well enough for two: Arthur Norton Hubbard Baxter.[256]

Not too long after they were married, Sarah went to live with them. The photograph of Sarah on her 65th birthday (31 January 1895) was taken "while she was living at 4 Pleasant Street in Quincy, Massachusetts."

Yet only a year and eleven days later, Sarah died – on 11 February 1896. She had packed a lot of living into her 66 years and eleven days. She is memorialized on her second husband's obelisk, so it seems reasonable to conclude her remains are buried near those of Richard and several other family members, in the cemetery of Zion Methodist Church in Freeland, Baltimore county, Maryland.

The marker is a rather stately obelisk with various names and dates on all sides. Perhaps Alfred Baxter, her son-in-law in the tombstone business produced this memorial.

But for those of us who have learned her story, her life stands as a memorial to a remarkable woman.

---

[256] ibid, Part Two, p. 12

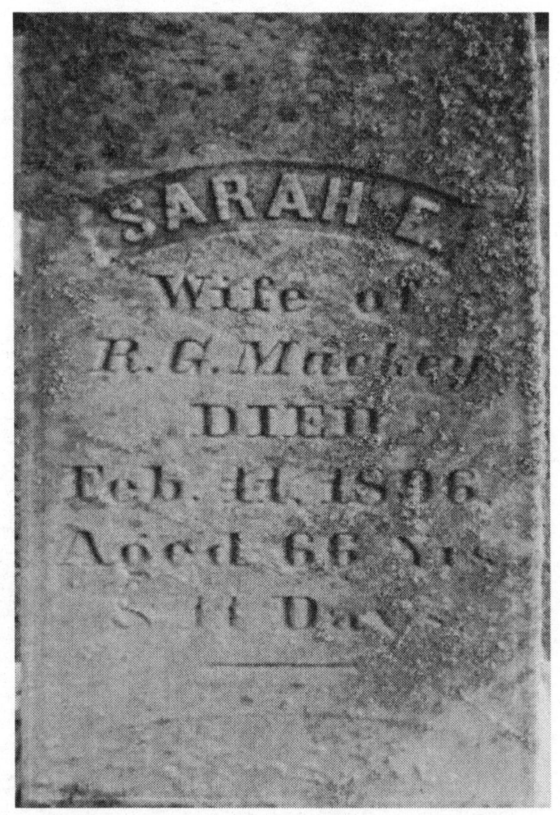

**Sarah E., wife of R.G. Mackey, memorial,
Zion Methodist Church, Freeland, Baltimore Co., MD**

AFTERWORD

This project has been more than thirty years in the writing, and I would be a liar if I didn't say I was glad to be done. There are far too many ramifications which rise from this "brief" tale - and had I known how hard it is to say no to any, I think I would have left it alone! But I am also glad I didn't leave it alone. I have learned a great deal, most all of it for my greater humility.

The story itself is to me chiefly about the intersection of mortality, faith and reason, the former a reality, the latter two necessities which are impossible to balance, but for the grace of God. And even when best balanced - we still don't know God's plans. My own application of these lessons is a desire to rest in that grace more diligently.

The process of research has been very humbling, too. Facts are very obscure things! For instance, trying to nail down what year what person on what boat did what at what point on the Missouri river is enough to drive one to absolute agnosticism. It seems that few if any of the old-timers felt it mattered to be accurate as to what year, place or even person they were reminiscing about. The resulting confusion eventually leads anyone "doing history" to some form of cynicism about the enterprise. I think of Jack Holterman, who spent so many years trying to unravel Alexander and Natawista's story amidst conflicting reports and recollections of their whereabouts at various times, and I could hear the weariness in his voice as he discussed the dilemmas.

The advantage of my project was the brevity of the central events, as referred to in the title. There's no doubt as to the year and months involved - although I can show you official Presbyterian histories and Montana historical publications that got those wrong, too! I must apologize to any more dedicated researcher who finds errors in my calendars. Such long-suffering persons patiently pan out the gold traces from lots and lots of gravel, and more power to them!

Apologies to anyone more knowledgeable who finds factual errors in this work. I have tried especially to attribute my information accurately to its earliest sources – but apologies for failures, there, too. A tremendous amount of fascinating material has NOT made its way into this book.

For instance – and I will include one more bit! One more curious bit of information to come my way– one that suddenly made me feel like the story had shifted into the literary genre of "magic realism," is a symbol and two notations I found on the oldest moderately accurate map we have of the Upper Missouri.

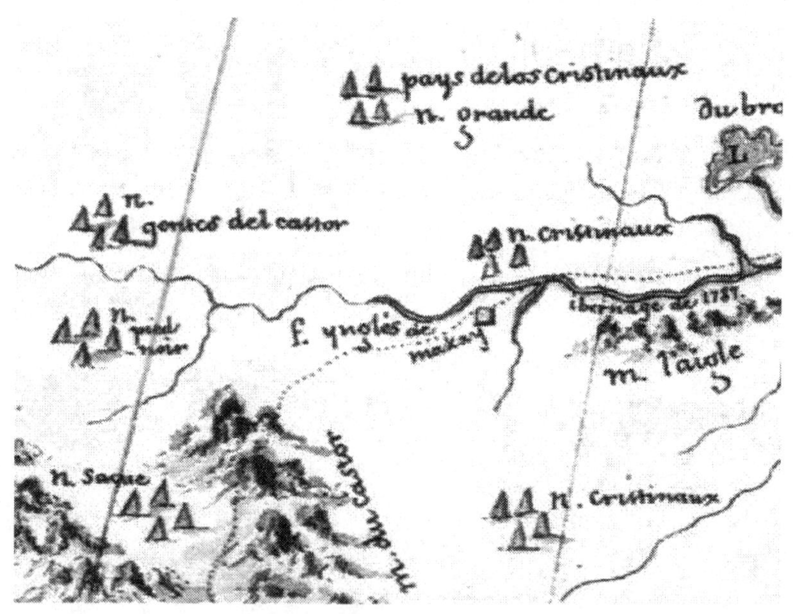

On this map, drafted in 1795, in the upper left corner, next to the French words "n. pied noir" ("the nation of the Blackfoots") is shown a square, and beneath it the notation *"f. ynglis de makay,"* which would seem to be "the English fort of Makay".

It turns out this map was drawn in 1795 by Antoine Pierre Soulard, the surveyor-general for Spanish officials in St. Louis nearly a decade before Lewis and Clark's transcontinental journey. Soulard knew of Fort Charles, a post built by one James Mackay near the Mandan villages on the Missouri. However the "Fort Makay" on Soulard's map is considerably north of the Missouri - on the North Saskatchewan river, and was an earlier post used by the same man. (The map is inaccurate to the extent that the east-west differential between the Mandan villages and "Fort Makay" near present Edmonton is actually much greater than shown.)

James Mackay's exploring partner, John Evans, was Welsh. Evans is famous for pursuing the possibility the Mandan Indians were remnants of the lost Welsh tribe of Prince Madoc. This tale had mythic origins and was recorded in the 1584 *Historie of Cambria* by David Powel, showing up thereafter in various forms, even as an argument in political justification of British annexation of North America. Evans and others claimed to find some evidence of Welsh connections, in blue eyes and light hair among the Mandans, but apparently no substantial similarities in the languages.

James Mackay, born in the northern Highlands of Scotland, was an early explorer of the Far West, but is best known for contributing to the drafting of the map of the Missouri river used by Lewis and Clark. Antoine Soulard, a good friend of Mackay made this map in 1795 showing Mackay's trip from the Saskatchewan River in Canada weaving through the Rocky Mountains and ending at the Mandan villages on the Missouri.

Mackay was the first person to write about the river he called "Rochejaune," that is, "Yellowstone," which has its sources in what became America's first national park.

Before the Louisiana Purchase, James Mackay worked for the Spanish and held the office of Captain-Commandant of the District of St. Charles which covered all the areas west of the Missouri River to the Rocky Mountains. After1804, he lived in St. Louis, becoming a Missouri Judge and State Legislator, and dying in 1822.

There is no known relationship between James Mackay and Elkanah Mackey, though their names are essentially the same, from the same Scottish root, a version of McHugh from the Gaelic, *MacAoidha*.

I knew none of this when I first came upon the notation on the map. It still tickles me that this map, which greatly helped Lewis and Clark, should include "Makay" written next to "the Blackfoot nation," although Elkanah did not come along until 61 years later.

BIBLIOGRAPHY

An Account of the Foreign Missions of the Presbyterian Church in the United States of America by Robert E. Speer, Secretary of the Board of Foreign Missions, Philadelphia, 1901. (Contains no reference to the Mackeys or George Smith)

"American Dinosaurs: Who and What Was First," by Keith Stewart Thomson copyright 2006 *Sigma Xi, The Scientific Research Society.* at: www.americanscientist.org.

American Indian Correspondence, Presbyterian Historical Society Collection of Missionary Letters 1833-1893. (microfilm) Greenwood Press, Inc. 51 Riverside Ave, Westport CT 06880.

American Missions in Bicentennial Perspective, Ed. R. Pierce Beaver. "The Churches and the Indians: Consequences of 350 Years of Missions" (Chapter 11). R. Pierce Beaver. USA: American Society of Missiology, 1977.

Annual report of the Commissioner of Indian Affairs, for the year 1856. US Govt. Published 1857.

Biographical Catalogue of Princeton Theological Seminary, 1815-1932. Compiled by Rev. Ed. Howell. Princeton, NJ: Trustees of the Theological Seminary of the Presbyterian Church, 1933.

A Biographical History of York County, Pennsylvania. John Gibson, editor. Clearfield Reprints, 1989.

The Blackfeet: Raiders on the Northwestern Plains. John Canfield Ewers. University of Oklahoma Press, 1958.

A Brief History of Lancaster County, With Special Reference To The Growth And Development of Its Institutions, Designed For The School And Home. Israel Smith Clare. Edited By Anna Lyle, Teacher of History In the Millersville State Normal School. Lancaster, PA:, Argus Pub. Co., 1892.

Collection of Missionary Letters, 1833-1893. Presbyterian Historical Society: Philadelphia. (microfilm - Presbyterian Historical Society American Indian Correspondence. Westport, CT: Greenwood Press, Inc.)

Collections of the Kansas State Historical Society, Vol 3, No. 1-4, Topeka: Kansas State Histrical Soceity, 1934.

Contributions to the Montana Historical Society, Vol 1. Helena, Rocky Mountain Publishing Company, 1876.

Contributions to the Montana Historical Society, Vol 6, 1907.

Contributions to the Montana Historical Society, Vol 8, 1917.

Contributions to the Montana Historical Society, Vol 9, 1923.

Contributions to the Montana Historical Society, Vol X, 1940.

"The Early Abolitionists of Lancaster County" by Thomas Whitson, Esq., in *Historical Papers and Addresses of the Lancaster County Historical Society, Volume 15* Lancaster County Historical Society, 1911.

Encyclopedia of Frontier Biography, Volume III,P-Z. Dan L. Thrapp. University of Nebraska Press, 1991.

Find-a-Grave online genealogical website, where I first found references to Sarah Armstrong Mackey's second marriage.

Foreign Missionary, The: Containing the Particular Accounts of the Foreign Missions of the Presbyterian Church, etc. July 1856 and January 1857 issues. Monthly magazine. Ed., Edward O. Jenkins. New York: Mission House.

Frontier Diplomats, Alexander Culbertson and Natoyist Siksina' Among the Blackfeet. Lesley Wischmann. Spokane, Wash., Arthur H. Clark Co., 2000. Univ. of Oklahoma, 2004.

The Fur Trade on the Upper Missouri 1840-1865. John E, Sunder. University of Oklahoma Press, 1993.

Great Falls Tribune. Newspaper, Great Falls, MT. Oct 5, 1985 issue.

Handbook of American Indians North of Mexico. Fred Webb Hodge. Bureau of American Ethnology, U.S. Govt. Printing Office, 1906.

An Historic Church: Makemie Memorial Presbyterian Church, Snow Hill, Md. Pamphlet. Mrs. Mary M. North. Snow Hill: Messenger Printing, 1904.

Historical Papers and Addresses of the Lancaster County Historical Society, Volume 15, especially "The Early Abolitionists of Lancaster County" by Thomas Whitson, Esq. Lancaster County Historical Society, Lancaster, PA, 1911.

History of Bedford, New Hampshire, from 1737: Being Statistics Compiled on the Occasion of the One Hundred and Fiftieth Anniversary of the Incorporation of the Town, May 15, 1900. Rumford Printing Company, 1903.

History of Lancaster County : with Biographical sketches. . . Franklin Ellis and Samuel Evans. Philadelphia, 1883.

History of Montana. 1739-1885: A History of Its Discovery and Settlement, Social and Commercial Progress, Mines and Miners, Agriculture and Stock-growing, Churches, Schools and Societies, Indians and Indian Wars, Vigilantes, Courts of Justice, Newspaper Press, Navigation, Railroads and Statistics, with Histories of Counties, Cities, Villages and Mining Camps . . .etc. Michael A. Leeson Chicago: Warner, Beers & Company, 1885.

A History of the Rock Presbyterian Church in Cecil County, Md. J. H. Johns. Oxford, PA: Oxford Press, 1872.

Holterman, Jack. "Little Dog," a monograph. (typescript given to author by Mr. Holterman)

Holterman, Jack. Letter correspondence with author, 1982-3.

Home and Foreign Record, The: of the Presbyterian Church in the USA, vol VII (1856), August & September issues. Monthly magazine. Boards of Missions, Education, Foreign Missions, and Publication, PC in USA. Philadelphia: Pub. House, 1856.

The Jesuits of the Middle United States, Vol 2 (of 3 vols.) Gilbert J. Garraghan, S.J. New York, NY: America Press, 1938.

Jim Bridger. J. Cecil Alter. University of Oklahoma Press, 2013.

Journal of Edwin A.C. Hatch, 1856. Quoted in various sources, including Montana Hist Soc. publications. Manuscript said to be in Newberry Library, Chicago.

Journal of the Department of History of the Presbyterian Church in the USA, Vol XIX, No. 8. "Missionary Endeavors of the Presbyterian Church Among the Blackfoot Indians in the 1850's." Guy S. Klett. Presbyterian Histrical Society, Dec 1941.

Kansas State Historical Society 8th Biennual Report. (for the period 1890-92). Kansas State Historical Society, 1892.

King of the High Missouri: The Saga of the Culbertsons. Jack Holterman. Billings and Helena: Falcon Press Pub. Co., 1987. (The original draft of this study of the Mackey's drew on a MS copy of the chapter, "Locust Grove" kindly given this author by Mr. Holterman, who then expected to publish it in Missoula, spring of 1984. That chapter ended up as three chapters – XVIIII-XX, in the published book.) Most relevant to this project is chapter XVIII "Zion Corners to the Great Falls," pp. 122-128.

Lowrie Bound Letterpress Book, Indian Missions Correspondence, Box A, vol 1. Walter Lowrie. Mission House, New York. Presbyterian Historical Society, Philadelphia.

The Mackey Family: 1729-1975. "Record of Robert Mackey and William Mackey and Their Descendants Who Lived Mostly in Pennsylvania and/or Maryland." Wilmer Mackey Sanner, compiler. Ellicott, MD, copyright 1974. 150 copies printed.

Memoirs of the Hon. Walter Lowrie. John Cameron Lowrie. New York: Baker, 1896.
The Mackeys (variously spelled) and allied families. Beatrice Mackey Doughtie. Decatur, Georgia : Bowen Press, Inc., 1957.

Memorials of Foreign Missionaries of the Presbyterian Church U.S.A. William Rankin, Late Treasurer of the Board of Foreign Missions. Presbyterian Board of Publication and Sabbath-school Work, Philadelphia, 1895.

Minutes, 1854-1866: Presbytery of Baltimore, PC in USA. Bound MSS. Philadelphia: Presbyterian Historical Society.

Minutes, Vol 3. (1858-1870): Presbytery of Lewes, PC in USA. Bound MSS. Philadelphia: Presbyterian Historical Society.

Minutes, 1837-1870, (Vol 1): Western Foreign Mission Society, New York Agency. Bound MSS. Philadelphia, Presbyterian Hist. Soc.

Minutes, General Assembly of the PC in USA, Vol XIV (1856). Philadelphia: Presbyterian Board of Publication, 1856.

Minutes, General Assembly of the PC in USA, Vol XV (1857). Philadelphia: Presbyterian Board of Publication, 1857.

Mission Among the Blackfeet. Howard L. Harrod. Norman: University of Oklahoma Press, 1971.

The Missouri Historical Review, State Historical Society of Missouri, Columbia, Missouri, Vol 62, Summer 1968. "Joseph LaBarge Steamboat Captain". T. S. Bowdern, S.J. (This article is reproduced on the Laberge-LaBarge Genealogy website with the permission of the State Historical Society of Missouri, 7/26/06.)

The Mountain Men and the Fur trade of the Far West, ed. Leroy R. Hafen. "James Kipp" by Ray H. Mattison. Arthur H Clark, Glendale, CA: 1966.

Nebraska Women in 1855. Harriet S. MacMurphy. Nebraska State Historical Society. (Read before the Society Jan. 12, 1897.)

Necrological Reports of Princeton Seminary, 1875-1889. Princeton, NJ. ?1889

North Dakota History, Journal of the Northern Plains, Vol. 77, Nos. 1 & 2. "James Kipp: Upper Missouri River Fur Trader and Missouri Farmer" by W. Raymond Wood. ND State Hist Soc., 2011.

One Hundred Years of Service By the Foreign Missionaries of Carlisle Presbytery, 1837-1937. Compiled by James Gray Rose, D.D. Mercersburg, PA, 1937.

Pioneer Reminiscences Transactions and Reports of the Nebraska State Historical Society 1 (1885): 25-85.{Transactions and Reports, Equivalent to Series 1-Volume 1}. Nebraska State Hist. Soc.

The Pioneer Work of the Presbyterian Church in Montana, ed. Geo. Edwards. Especially, p 14, "Sketch of the Beginning of Presbyterianism in Montana, " by Rev. Thomas V. Moore, D.D. Independent Publishing Co., 1907.

The Presbyterian, September 18, 1858. Denominational newspaper. "Melancholy Intelligence": article by Heaton, Rev. A. C. dated September 10, 1858, Princess Anne, MD.

Presbyterian Church in the USA Board of Foreign Missions: Missions Correspondence and Reports, vol. 4 (Africa Letters, 1850-1860) of 16 original volumes. (Also on microfilm and indexed as Foreign Missions Papers, Calendar, vol. 1 (Miscellaneous and Africa). Philadelphia: Presbyterian Historical Society.

Presbyterian Historical Almanac and Annual Remembrancer of the Church, Volume 2, for 1859-1860. Edited by Joseph M. Wilson. Philadelphia, 1860. "Mackey, Elkanah D. "

Presbyterian Historical Almanac and Annual Remembrancer of the Church, Volume 10 , for 1868. Edited by Joseph M. Wilson. Philadelphia, 1868.

Presbyterians and the Negro: A History. Andrew E. Murray, Philadelphia: Presbyterian Historical Society, 1966.

Proceedings of the Academy of Natural Science, viii, Phila., 1856. "Various notices of fossil remains of fish, reptiles, and mammals, etc. discovered by Dr. F.V. Hayden in the Bad Lands of the Judith River, Nebraska Territory." (Some of Hayden's reports also published in *Amer. Jour. Sci.* xxi and xxii.)

Proceedings of the Academy of Science and Letters of Sioux City. Sioux City, published by the Academy, 1904-1906. 2 vol.

Record, vol. 8 (1845-1864); Presbytery of New Castle, PC in USA. Bound MSS. Philadelphia, Presbyterian Historical Society.

The River Press, Fort Benton, MT. A weekly newspaper. "Building Mackinaw in 1856 Required Much Manpower," July 29, 1981 issue, and other articles as per footnotes. Editor Overholser was an historian of the Upper Missouri and early Montana.

Smithsonian Institution, Bureau of American Ethnology, Bulletin 147. John Francis McDermott, editor. "Journal of an Expedition to the Mauvaises Terres and the Upper Missouri in 1850," by Thaddeus A. Culbertson. U.S. Govt. Print. Office, 1952.

Steamboats on Western Rivers. An Economic and Technological History. Louis C. Hunter, Beatrice Jones Hunter. Courier Corporation, 1949.

Terrible Justice: Sioux Chiefs and U.S. Soldiers on the Upper Missouri, 1854–1868. Doreen Chaky. U. of Oklahoma Press, 2014

Then and now; or, Thirty-six years in the Rockies: Personal reminiscences of some of the first pioneers of the state of Montana. Indians and Indian wars. The past and present of the Rocky mountain country, 1864-1900. Robert Vaughn. Minneapolis, Tribune printing company, 1900.

This Far-off Wild Land: The Upper Missouri Letters of Andrew Dawson . by Lesley Wischmann and Andrew Erskine Dawson. Norman, Univ. of Oklahoma Press, 2013.

Transactions of the Kansas State Historical Society, 1905-1906, Vol 9, especially "Missouri River Steamboats," list compiled by Phillip E. Chappell. Topeka, 1906.

Travels in the Interior of North America, 1832-1834, Volume 1. Maximilian von Wied. Arthur H. Clark Company, 1905.

United States Pacific Rail Road Expedition and Surveys - 47th & 49th Parallels, Report, 1853. Isaac Stevens. Lithographs: Sarony Major & Knapp Liths. 449 Broadway, N.Y.

Vanguard of Expansion: Army Engineers in the Trans-Mississippi West, 1819-1879 by Frank N. Schubert. United States. Army. Corps of Engineers. Historical Division, 1980.

The War Against Pro-slavery Religion: Abolitionism and the Northern Churches, 1830-1965 John R. McKivigan. Ithaca NY: Cornell U Press, 1984.

Way's Packet Directory, 1848-1983: Passenger Steamboats of the Mississippi River System since the Advent of Photography in Mid-Continent America; Captain Frederick Way, Jr. Ohio University Press, 1983 and 1994. (My father, corresponded with Captain Way, in re Missouri River steamboats. He, James Edwards Trott, painted many of them in Upper Missouri settings.)

ILLUSTRATIONS & SOURCES

Frontispiece & Cover – photo and retouched photo portrait of Elkanah and Sarah Mackey, circa 1856, from *The Mackey Family* by Wilmer Mackey Sanner, and by kind permission of Peter Parlette.

p. 4 -- Michael Simpson Culbertson, . China Missionary and Alexander's brother Courtesy of Presbyterian Historical Society.

p. 6 - Brief article in *The Foreign Missionary*, about the Blackfoot Mission. Presbyterian missions magazine, 1856. Courtesy of Presbyterian Historical Society.

p. 9 - Sarah Martin Mackey, Elkanah's mother, and wife of William Mackey. . From *The Mackey Family* by Wilmer Mackey Sanner. By kind permission of Peter Parlette.

p. 15 – Elkanah Dare Mackey's signature.

p. 18 – Walter Lowrie, Secretary, Foreign Missions Board. Courtesy of Presbyterian Historical Society.

p. 24 – Group of Piegan Indians, from a painting so titled by John Mix Stanley, 1867. Original painting in Denver Public Library, Denver, Colorado.

p. 26 - Alexander Culbertson from a portrait by John James Audubon and Isaac Sprague. In Holterman's *King of the High Missouri,* courtesy of Kerrigan Family Trust.

p. 27 – Walter Lowrie's signature

p. 29 -- Father Pierre-Jean De Smet (1801-1873) A portion of an 1863 photo, one of the few known from Gustavus Sohon's studio in San Francisco. For the full photo see *King of the High Missouri,* Jack Holterman, 1987, where it is reproduced from one held by Montana Historical Society.

p. 33 – Alexander Culbertson, small section from a sketch by Rudolph Friederich Kurz. Kurz was a Swiss painter and writer who spent the years 1846-50 traveling along the Mississippi and

Missouri rivers. After 1850 for several years he worked as a clerk for the American Fur Company while sketching and painting on the Upper Missouri.

p. 38 - A Buffalo Hunt, from a lithograph: "Blackfeet Indians – Three Buttes" by John Mix Stanley, in Isaac Stevens' 1853 Pacific Railroad Report, *U.S.P.R.R. Exp. & Surveys - 47th & 49th Parallels*/ General Report / Plate XXVII - Stanley, Del./ Sarony Major & Knapp Liths. 449 Broadway, N.Y.

p. 54 - Bellevue Baptist Mission from an engraving after Karl Bodmer, artist who accompanied naturalist, Maximilian von Wied to the Upper Missouri, 1832-34. This Indian mission came to an end, but a few years later the Presbyterians started theirs nearby. Here the Mackeys waited for the steamboat that took them the rest of the way to Montana.

p. 65 - Alexander Culbertson, portrait painted by John Mix Stanley circa 1854, probably while Culbertson was in Washington, D.C., lobbying on behalf of American Fur Company, from Leslie Wischmann's *Frontier Diplomats*, courtesy of Idaho State Historical Society. Now belonging to and reproduced here by courtesy of the River and Plains Society, Fort Benton, MT.

p. 66 - Alfred Jefferson Vaughan, Blackfoot Agent 1857, photo of him later as a Confederate Brigadier General in the Civil War.

p. 71 - Andrew Dawson, American Fur Company employee and Factor at Fort Benton from 1854.

p. 74 -- Gouverneur Kemble Warren, a lieutenant in the Army Corps of Topographical Engineers under General Harney in 1856, whose expeditions culminated in the first full map of the western United States in 1858. This photo taken during the Civil War when he was a Major General in the Union Army. Referred to as the "Hero of Little Roundtop" for his part at Gettysburg—with three other men who are variously afforded that title.

p. 75 – Fort Pierre, taken from an 1854 watercolor by Frederick Behman. Original watercolor in State Archives of the South

Dakota State Historical Society. Courtesy of South Dakota State Historical Society

p. 76 -- Ferdinand Vandeveer Hayden, discoverer of the first American dinosaur remains to be formally described – which he found in 1855 in the "Badlands" of the Judith River. They were described by Joseph Leidy in Philadelphia in 1856.

p. 77 -- F. V. Hayden's signature

p. 78 – Lieut. G.K. Warren's signature

p. 84 - Captain Joseph La Barge, Master of the *St. Mary.* From T. S. Bowdern, S.J. article, " Joseph LaBarge Steamboat Captain, 2006. Courtesy of State Historical Society of Missouri.

p. 87 - Mrs. Culbertson, "Natawista" and child, from a portrait by John James Audubon and Isaac Sprague. In Holterman's King of the High Missouri, courtesy of Kerrigan Family Trust.

p. 90 - .Fort Union, from a lithograph, by John Mix Stanley, in Isaac Stevens' 1853 Pacific Railroad Report. *U.S.P.R.R. Exp. & Surveys - 47th & 49th Parallels*/ General Report / Plate XVI - Stanley, Del./ Sarony Major & Knapp Liths. 449 Broadway, N.Y.

p. 92 - Indian Agent Alfred J. Vaughan's signature

p. 94 - Jim Bridger, noted mountain man. A copy of this photo in State Archives of South Dakota State Historical Society. Courtesy of South Dakota State Historical Society.

p. 102 – Part of a photograph said to be of Mrs. Culbertson, Natawista, but now thought to be of her daughter, Fanny . In Jack Holterman's *King of the High Missouri* by permission of Mollie F. Culbertson Sedgwick.

p. 105 - Facsimile from Elkanah's Report of section concerning Sarah's Reception among the Indians. Courtesy of Presbyterian Historical Society.

p. 111 – The Overland Route, Map One, from Fort Union west along Milk River, 26 July through 6 August 1856. Copyright 2016 James H. Trott.

p. 119 – Milk River near Junction of Missouri, from a lithograph by John Mix Stanley, in Isaac Stevens' 1853 Pacific Railroad

Report. *U.S.P.R.R. Exp. & Surveys - 47th & 49th Parallels/* General Report/Plate XVIII - Stanley, Del./ Sarony Major & Knapp Liths. 449 Broadway, N.Y.

p. 121 – The Overland Route, Map Two, from Milk River to Fort Benton, 7 August through 15 July 1856. Copyright, James H. Trott.

p. 127 - John Mix Stanley's depiction of Fort Benton, in Isaac Stevens' 1853 Pacific Railroad Report. *U.S.P.R.R. Exp. & Surveys - 47th & 49th Parallels/* General Report/Plate XXIV - Stanley, Del./ Sarony Major & Knapp Liths. 449 Broadway, N.Y.

p. 128 - Fort Benton, 1866. From a photo in *King of the High Missouri,* Jack Holterman. Courtesy of the Montana Historical Society.

p. 134 – The Marias River, from a lithograph by John Mix Stanley in Isaac Stevens' 1853 Pacific Railroad Report. *U.S.P.R.R. Exp. & Surveys - 47th & 49th Parallels/* General Report/ Plate XXVI - Stanley, Del./ Sarony Major & Knapp Liths. 449 Broadway, N.Y.

p. 137 –: Blackfoot Treaty Council, 1855, From a drawing by Gustavus Sohon. Washington State Historical Society, Tacoma.

p. 148 - Mackinaw on the Missouri from an aquatint "Encampment of the Travelers (on the Missouri)" by Outhwaite based on a Karl Bodmer watercolor from a drawing Bodmer made during the fall of 1833 as he travelled with Maximilian von Wied.

p. 151 - Ne-Tannay, The Only Chief, or Stam-yehk-sas-ci-cay, Lame Bull, Piegan Chief, from a sketch by Gustavus Sohon, 1855.

p. 160 – Facsimile of first page of Elkanah's 1856 Report to the Presbyterian Foreign Missions Board, written in St. Joseph during the Mackey's return from Fort Benton. Courtesy of Presbyterian Historical Society.

p. 165 – Facsimile of section of Elkanah's Report praising Mr. Culbertson. Courtesy of Presbyterian Historical Society.

p. 176 – Photograph of plaque commemorating Elkanah and his brother William in Makemie Memorial Presbyterian Church, Snow Hill, MD. Photo: James H. Trott.

p. 182 – Alexander Culbertson signature.

p. 184 – Facsimile of Walter Lowrie's last letter to Alexander Culbertson. Courtesy of Presbyterian Historical Society.

p. 185 - Office of Indian Affairs 1857 letter to Walter Lowrie, written by Charles E. Mix. (Gist of the letter: any decision regarding federal funding of a Presbyterian Blackfoot school is to be put off until the next administration takes office.)

p. 186 – From a photo of Alexander Culbertson in *Fort Union and Its Neighbors on the Upper Missouri : A Chronological Record of Events* by Frank B. Harper, pamphlet of the Great Northern Railway: "photo by courtesy of Charles M. Kessler, Helena, Montana." This undated pamphlet was a special publication made for the Great Northern's Upper Missouri Historical Expedition in July 1925, commemorating western explorers. Photo apparently from James Willard Schultz Photographs, 1859-1947, now held in Merrill G. Burlingame Special Collections at Montana State University Libraries.

p. 193 – Natawista Culbertson, circa 1859, from a photo in Lesley Wischmann's book *Frontier Diplomats*, by courtesy of Natawista's great-grandson, George H.R. Taylor, Bethesda, MD. Used here with the permission of the Taylor family, Bethesda.

p. 197 - Elkanah and Julie Anna Mackey Table-tomb/grave, Makemie Memorial Church cemetery, Snow Hill, MD. Photo: James H. Trott.

p. 198 – The horizontal gravestone over Elkanah and Julia Anna Mackay's graves, Makemie Memorial Church cemetery, Snow Hill, MD. Photo: James H. Trott.

p. 204 -- Richard Guthrie Mackey, Sarah's second husband. From *The Mackey Family* by Wilmer Mackey Sanner. By kind permission of Peter Parlette.

p. 209 -- Richard Guthrie Mackey's gravestone, Freeland, MD. From a photo courtesy of James Mayfield on Find-A-Grave website.

p. 211 -- Sarah Armstrong Mackey on her 65th Birthday. From *The Mackey Family* by Wilmer Mackey Sanner. By kind permission of Peter Parlette.

p. 213-- Sarah Armstrong Mackey's gravestone , Freeland, MD. From a photo courtesy of James Mayfield on Find-A-Grave website.

p. 216 – Black & white version of a small section from Antoine Pierre Soulard's 1795 map. showing the "*f. ynglis de makay*" on the North Saskatchewan in Blackfoot country.

APPRECIATIONS

I would like to express particular appreciation to the following people who were of great help in my pursuit of the history of Elkanah and Sarah Mackey:

To the memory of my father, James Edwards Trott, who always made Montana history live - whether in his words, his enthusiasm, or his paintings. And to my mother Lucile Hanford Trott and her stillborn books.

To the memory of Mr. Joel F. Overholser, Editor and Editor Emeritus of the *River Press*, Fort Benton, whose research and knowledge (if not his style) inspired much interest in history. He it was who first drew my attention to the Mackey story.

To the memory of Mr. Jack Holterman, whom I first met and corresponded with during research for a novel I have yet to publish. Jack's *King of the High Missour,i* one of the fullest accounts of Alexander Culbertson, including information about Presbyterian missionary Michael Simpson Culbertson.

To the Presbyterian Historical Society staff during my research in the early 1980s: Gerald Gillette, manager of Research and Library Services, Mary Plummer, Barbara Roy and especially Norotha Robinson and Martha Thomas, who showed me the intricacies of the collection and located and copied various documents.

Special thanks to Lily Sanner, Edith Sanner Parlette, and Peter Parlette who gave me permission to use the information from Wilmer Mackey Sanner's book, while Peter also showed me additional material.

To the Taylor Family of Bethesda, MD, for permission to use Natawista's photo from Leslie Wischmann's book.

To Leslie Wischmann, herself, who kindly answered a number of important questions, both in her *Frontier Diplomats* and in phone conversation.

To Ken Robison of the River and Plains Society, Fort Benton, for taking the time to discuss this project.

To Tom Sorkness who weeded out several dozen errors, and gave me valuable suggestions, such as the need for maps.

To Kimiko and Garrett, who put us up and put up with us during research expeditions to Maryland.

And finally to Roseann, who is not only the best reader and critic of all I write – but also of the author.

James Howard Trott, August 2016

Made in the USA
Middletown, DE
16 October 2016